SIT!
THE COMPLETE GUIDE TO A WELL BEHAVED, WELL CARED FOR DOG

SIT!

THE COMPLETE GUIDE TO A WELL BEHAVED, WELL CARED FOR DOG

Angela Sayer

TREASURE PRESS

CONTENTS

First published in Great Britain in 1982 by
Octopus Books Limited
This edition published in 1987 by
Treasure Press
59 Grosvenor Street
London W1
© 1982 Hennerwood Publications Limited
Reprinted 1988
ISBN 1 85051 197 7
Printed in Hong Kong

Picture captions
Half-title page:
All dogs, except guide dogs, must be trained to wait patiently outside shops.

Title spread:
Young children and puppies soon learn mutual respect.

Contents spread:
Big dogs enjoy invigorating country walks.

A Dog in the Family

Choosing your dog

The dog is said to be man's best friend; it is certainly his oldest, being the first of all animals to accept domestication. Since those long-ago days the dog has undergone many physiological changes, although its behaviour patterns seem to have remained remarkably constant. From the beginning of his association with dogs, Stone Age man began to select them for specific purposes, choosing those with the most aggressive tendencies to act as guards, while those that responded most readily to training were encouraged to help in tending semi-wild flocks and herds of cattle. As the generations passed, man increasingly used the dog as aid and companion, selectively breeding animals for hunting, guarding, fighting, and haulage. Eventually, dogs also became pets and were then bred to fix unusual or particularly appealing characteristics, such as diminutive size and the foreshortened face now known to elicit the mothering response in humans.

It is important to examine your reasons for wanting a dog. When you have decided to go ahead and buy one, it is equally important to ensure that you select the right breed or type to suit your temperament and life-style. You must also decide from the outset whether you want a pedigree or a mongrel, an adult or a puppy, a dog or a bitch, and whether you should have one dog or two. You must remember that a dog is highly dependent on you, its owner, and that you will be responsible for it for the span of its life. It is grossly unfair to expect a dog to change its established home for a new one unless this is unavoidable owing to extreme, unforeseen circumstances.

Life expectancy in dogs varies considerably, with a mean average of 10 years. Medium-sized dogs seem to live the longest; very large and very tiny breeds have the shortest spans. Obviously, good feeding and fitness help to prolong the life, just as bad diets and obesity can help to shorten it.

Before looking at available dogs you must ask yourself how and where you will house and exercise it. You must decide how much money you can afford each year on outgoings, which will include vaccinations and veterinary fees, a licence, grooming equipment, collars and leads, baskets and bowls, and possibly boarding kennels and

Pages 6–7 The Boxer makes an ideal family pet, always game for a romp or country walk, and develops a protective relationship with children.

training fees, as well as food. You must be prepared to have regular sessions every day for feeding, grooming, exercise, training, and play; and if you are taking on a young puppy, you must be tolerant of some degree of playful damage and accidents in the early days.

Pedigree or mongrel?

In deciding between a pedigree and a mongrel there are several factors you must take into account. A pedigree puppy will cost more than a mongrel, but it will grow according to its breed standards so that you can be sure of its eventual adult size, shape, and coat texture. You will also have a fair idea of the sort of character and behaviour to expect and the amount of work you will have to devote to grooming and exercise. Some pedigree dogs, however, have been bred into shapes which are contrary to nature's design, and these may need special care and attention to keep them in good health.

Mongrels are dogs of unknown ancestry, and the adult animal may bear little resemblance to the puppy from which it developed or to its mother. Mongrel puppies are generally very

Adult or puppy?

It is always better to buy a puppy than a full-grown dog as a family pet, for, although you will have the problems of house-training and the basic lessons to instil, as the puppy grows up it will fit readily into your home life. Taking on an older dog can present difficulties; it may have set patterns of behaviour which are unacceptable to you but which are impossible to change. Some adult dogs, however, really *need* new homes, through no fault of their own, and you may be lucky enough to get a perfect pet; owners die or emigrate, for instance, and a perfectly healthy and well-behaved dog may find itself in need of a new owner. Other adult dogs, however, are passed on from home to home because, owing to lack of early training or general care, they have become intolerable to their owners. Unfortunately, it often proves impossible to rehabilitate such animals no matter how much love, care, and attention their new owners give them. If you do decide to take on an adult dog, try to arrange for this to be on a trial basis for a period of a week to 10 days so that you can be certain that it will settle down and become a happy and acceptable pet in your home.

Dog or bitch?

The sex of your dog is very important too, for dogs and bitches have quite different temperaments. For would-be owners with little experience in dog keeping, and for those with young children, the choice should always be a bitch. She will need far less discipline than a dog and will fit much more readily into the natural hierarchy of the family unit. Some male dogs do integrate perfectly well with the family structure, but the relationship between the male dog and its owner is far more intense than that which exists with a bitch, and the male dog has a built-in aggressiveness related directly to its sexuality.

The degree of intimacy achieved by the man:dog relationship reflects similarities within their social orders of family and pack. In this relationship the human family takes the place of the pack for the dog; but even so it is beneficial to have more than one dog if you can afford them. It is best of all to have two bitches, as these will get along well together with only the occasional squabble. Two male dogs may be kept safely together if they are of one of the more placid-natured breeds; but other males may be inclined to fight, especially those of the terrier group.

cheap to buy, but in the long run they may cost just as much to keep as a pedigree dog of the same size.

Many mongrels prove to be highly intelligent and make good family dogs, and as they are cross-bred they rarely show any hereditary defects. It is sometimes possible to buy first-cross puppies, either from a mis-mating or from a mating that was intended to combine the characteristics of two breeds. If such puppies combine the best traits of both parents, the results can be delightful; but they are equally likely to combine the less-desirable characteristics.

It is an exciting day when the new puppy is brought home for the first time, but remember not to let it walk in public places before it has completed its course of vaccinations against canine diseases. Note the way its young owner supports the puppy with his left hand.

Keeping one dog and one bitch can pose problems, especially during the twice-yearly oestrous cycle of the bitch.

Breed?

There are so many breeds of pedigree dog that it can be confusing in the extreme when you come to decide on the right sort to choose. To help you make up your mind we have drawn up a directory (page 66) of the most suitable breeds and their attributes. The Kennel Club of Great Britain divides dogs into two main categories, Sporting and Non-Sporting. The first group contains all the hounds, gundogs, and terriers, while the second group covers guarding, herding, and watch dogs, companions, and the tiny toy dogs.

Most of the gundogs are very lively and energetic and need a lot of exercise to maintain their lean, hard condition. Some of the varieties which carry feather-long silky hair on their legs and tail also have long hair on their pendulous ears, and need more attention and grooming than the short-coated strains. Few gundogs make good guards, but most of them are superb with children. The terriers are very varied in appearance; many are named after the regions in which they were originally developed to hunt and kill vermin. They are all basically similar in temperament – very quick, agile, and alert, with fast reactions which can cause them to snap first and ask questions later. The smooth terriers need little grooming, but the wiry coated ones may need regular hand-stripping or trimming – a

job for the expert. The various scent hounds rarely make good family pets: they are pack animals by nature and most of them crave the freedom to run all day. Sight hounds such as the Afghan and Saluki can be very aloof and retain a strong hunting instinct; like all the hounds they need lots of exercise.

The Non-Sporting Group is divided into various sub-groups. In the Working section are popular breeds such as the German Shepherd Dog (often called Alsatian), Collies, Corgies, the Boxer, guard dogs such as the Rottweiler and Dobermann Pinscher, and the giant Newfoundland, St Bernard, Pyrenean Mountain Dog, and Great

Dane. Another section, known as the Utility Group, covers breeds such as the popular Poodle, the Dalmatian, and the Bulldog. The Toy Group has a wide range of tiny dogs ranging from the minute Chihuahua up to the fairly robust Cavalier King Charles Spaniel.

From such an enormous selection of breeds you will almost certainly find the perfect dog for your family. Having decided on the breed, you must now find a suitable puppy to purchase.

How to find your puppy

Puppies are advertised in the classified columns of local and national newspapers as well as in dog journals and magazines dealing with country sports and other pursuits. Cards are often placed in newsagents' windows, pet shops, and on notice boards outside country kennels. The Kennel Club is the governing body for all pedigree-dog business and deals with all aspects of breed recording and registrations. Founded in 1873 under the patronage of the Prince of Wales (later King Edward VII), it is situated in Clarges Street, London W1. You may write to

the Kennel Club for its list of breed clubs (enclose a self-addressed and correctly stamped envelope for the reply). When you have the breed-club lists you can write to the secretaries of the breeds you have short-listed asking for further information and details of members who may have puppies for sale. Most club secretaries work in an honorary capacity, giving up hours of their spare time, so it is better to write to them rather than to telephone. Enclose a self-addressed, stamped envelope approximately A5 in size in case there are breed information sheets or newsletters to be mailed back to you.

Choosing your puppy

Virtually all puppies are irresistibly attractive and it is fatally easy to buy on impulse, so before you go shopping for your dog you should make some contingency plans and stick to them rigidly. Do *not* take any family, friends, or children with you: it is easy to be swayed into buying a puppy for the wrong reasons, and children are renowned for selecting the smallest, shyest, and often the weakest pup in the litter. You should buy directly from the breeder, if possible, rather than from a dealer, pet-store, or market. In this way you will be able to see the

Choose your puppy by selecting from the litter, and with the expert advice of an experienced breeder. Cocker Spaniel pups are irresistible.

whole litter and the mother as well as the conditions in which the puppies have been raised. Some breeders also keep their own stud dog, so you may be allowed to see the puppies' father too, and in this way assure yourself of the family tendencies as regards size, conformation, and temperament. Most breeders have the good of their puppies at heart and will give you sound advice on feeding, rearing, and general care.

Choosing a puppy from the litter is not as simple as it sounds. It is all too easy to be influenced by factors that owe more to sentimentality than to sense. The smallest and weakest pup in a litter may look the most appealing, but it might require a great deal of attention and veterinary help during rearing. It is quite a good idea to choose the puppy that first comes to you (if it is of the right sex). The puppies in the litter should look healthy and clean and not smell too 'doggy'. There should be no signs of discharge from the eyes or nostrils (some breeders may try to excuse these symptoms by saying they are due to sawdust or bedding). The ears should be spotless inside and the teeth should be sharp and white. Healthy puppies are plump, but without the extreme pot-bellied effect that could indicate a heavy worm burden. The skin should be very mobile and seemingly too large for the puppy's frame. The skin should be clean without any sign of soreness or redness anywhere, particularly under the belly or between the thighs, and there should be no black specks indicating the presence of

fleas. Look under the tail for any staining – a sign of diarrhoea – and examine the umbilicus area for any sign of a hernia. If the breed requires docking of the tail and removal of the dewclaws (the rudimentary fifth digit on the inside of the leg), check to see that this has been done correctly. Make sure that you see your chosen puppy running around and that it moves soundly. If you arrive during the litter's sleep period, be prepared to wait until the pups have had a chance to wake up properly – after a long sleep it takes some minutes before their natural bounce returns.

When you buy a pure-bred puppy, the breeder will provide you with a copy of its pedigree, which is a written list of its ancestry going back some four or five generations. The puppy may have been registered with the Kennel Club, in which case you will also have a certificate to enable its particulars to be officially transferred to your ownership.

Buying a pup with a pedigree does not necessarily mean that you acquire a show-dog. If you do eventually hope to show or breed, you must make this quite clear to the breeder from the outset. High-quality puppies with show potential may cost several times more than a pedigree pup of only pet potential. It is in the breeder's interests to sell you the puppy most suitable for your needs. If you just want a healthy, happy pet, do not pay the extra money for one which excels in all physical features; it is equally pointless to buy a standard puppy if you hope to win top prizes.

If you do decide to go in for a show-dog, you may have to wait longer for your puppy. The reason is that the breeder may decide that he needs to 'run on' several of the puppies for a few months before he will be able to be certain that they are of show standard. Naturally, this will increase the purchase price, but it is worth it if you want to win in competition.

Preparing the new home

It is important to select and arrange the purchase of your puppy before it is ready to leave its mother, so that you will have time to prepare your home for its arrival. A young puppy will chew everything within reach, so it is vital to provide a safe, suitable environment for its first few weeks in your home. Most people find one end of the kitchen to be the ideal site for the puppy's bed; one way is to partition an area with a mesh pen, a wire fireguard, or a baby's discarded playpen. Be sure to remove all potential hazards such as electric flex and anything that can be chewed and swallowed.

You can make a suitable bed for your puppy from a sturdy grocery carton lined with an old sweater or blanket. It should be just large enough for the puppy to lie on its side comfortably; if it is any larger it will fail to give the necessary feeling of security. As the box becomes chewed or soiled, it can be easily replaced with a new one. It is pointless to provide young puppies with smart wicker baskets, as these are almost made to be chewed.

The puppy will need its own bowls and dishes, of a design suitable for its breed so that it can eat and drink comfortably without getting its nose or ears submerged. You must make sure that your garden is safely fenced in and that the gates shut securely and automatically. Swimming pools and fish ponds must be protected until the pup understands the dangers: although most dogs can swim naturally, they cannot clamber out up steep sides and might drown through exhaustion.

The puppy will not need a collar or lead at first, as it should be carried everywhere outside its home base until its vaccination programme is complete; you should arrange to collect it by car rather than by public transport, which could prove to be a health risk. You are sure to want to buy toys for your puppy

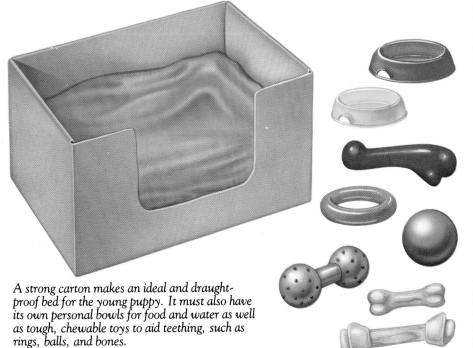

A strong carton makes an ideal and draught-proof bed for the young puppy. It must also have its own personal bowls for food and water as well as tough, chewable toys to aid teething, such as rings, balls, and bones.

Right *The young puppy is an inquisitive little animal, and quickly learns to find its way around its new home and garden. It should be allowed to spend much of its playtime in the fresh air.*

to help to alleviate boredom. Make sure that you purchase only specially made dog toys such as rawhide chews, a hard rubber ball too large to be swallowed, and a substantial toy with an exciting squeaker inside. You will need lots of newspaper, a supply of kitchen paper towelling, and a supply of food as recommended by the breeder. In winter a stone hot-water bottle wrapped in a warm blanket helps to comfort the puppy during its first lonely nights, and some people believe that a loudly ticking clock placed by the pup's bed soothes the little animal and induces sleep.

The puppy's new world

When you bring your puppy home for the first time you should bear in mind that this is one of the most unsettling and frightening experiences of its life. It is leaving its family and familiar surroundings and is being subjected to a bewildering variety of new scents, sights, and sounds. If it is travelling by car it may well be sick, so be sure to wrap it well in a warm towel or blanket and have plenty of newspapers and soft kitchen tissue with you on the journey. Get home as quickly and smoothly as possible, holding the puppy close for comfort and talking to it in a soothing voice. The breeder will not have fed the puppy before its collection, so on arrival home you may offer it a small milk and cereal feed.

In your home the puppy will feel lost and very vulnerable at first and you must give it sufficient sympathy and understanding to instil confidence and trust. If it accepts the cereal feed, well and good; if it refuses it and whines, wrap the puppy in its blanket and place it in the prepared box to sleep. If it cries, give it a comforting cuddle before putting it back to bed. It is best to have collected your puppy early in the day so that you can spend a few hours helping it to settle in before nightfall. At this stage the pup's play periods are about half an hour long, interspersed with long sleep sessions. Regular routines must be enforced from the beginning.

Night time can pose problems at first, for the new puppy will probably cry, whimper, and whine, hating to be left alone. Try putting the well-wrapped stone hot-water bottle in its bed; you may find the deeply ticking clock will have a soothing effect too, sounding as it does like a steady heart beat.

Puppies and playmates

It is not advisable to buy a puppy if there is a very young child in the house. A toddler spends a lot of time crawling

Having introduced a new puppy to an older family dog, care must be exercised to ensure that neither becomes over-excited in play. Dogs use their teeth in mock-fighting forms of play, but rarely hurt one another when carefully supervised.

around and playing on the floor, and a young puppy is not the most hygienic of playmates. Older children, however, are quickly taught the importance of hand-washing and they are better able to understand the simple rules for playing and helping with the family pet.

A healthy puppy is naturally playful and full of fun and is bound to enjoy playing with children. Short periods of deep recuperative sleep following play sessions are essential for the puppy's correct growth pattern, so children must be taught to respect these times. Do not allow the puppy to become exhausted or overheated and too excited during play. Take great care to see that it does not slip awkwardly at speed or try to climb onto or jump down from high furniture. Children must learn that a puppy will chew just about anything it can find, and will swallow any object small enough to pass down its throat, often with unfortunate consequences. They must not be allowed to smack the puppy, pull it around on a lead, or in any way treat it as a toy.

If it is necessary to carry the puppy, hold it carefully with two arms encompassing both the fore and hindlimbs to give control and support. Never pick it up by the forelimbs or by the scruff of the neck. If children are allowed to tease the puppy, aggressive behaviour may become instilled in the animal and could be difficult to change later on. The children should help to groom the little dog and get it used to having its ears, mouth, paws, and tail examined and handled without causing any fuss. Do not allow children to feed sweets and tit-bits to the puppy, but do encourage them to help keep its bedding tidy, change the water in its bowl and help prepare its meals.

Even greater care is required in introducing an adult dog into a household with children. The animal may have deep-rooted behaviour patterns which must be watched for, and its moods should be respected. A bitch is much more easily absorbed into a normal household than a male dog, but most well-brought-up dogs soon adjust to new routines if given sufficient time, understanding and affection.

An older dog generally accepts the arrival of a new human baby with interest and tolerance, but it is impor-

It takes a little time for young kittens and puppies to become friends. If they are carefully introduced and their early encounters are supervised, they will soon make perfect playmates.

tant to prevent feelings of jealousy arising. Bitches are often very inquisitive about babies; allowing them to sniff and examine a soiled napkin seems to help them understand the strange new and helpless creature. Some normally docile bitches become extremely protective and even refuse to allow strangers or visitors near the baby's pram.

Introducing a new puppy to other household pets can be difficult, and care must be taken not to upset the established animals. The easiest way to allow a new puppy to meet an older family dog is to make the introduction in the garden. Holding it on its lead, make a great fuss of the older dog then bring the puppy forward. After sniffing each other thoroughly they may start an excited form of play, but do not let this get out of hand. If they seem to get along quite well let the older dog loose and encourage them both to follow you into the house. In this way, the dog will feel that it has made the decision to bring the puppy to you. If the ruse

works, you will have taken the first major step to success. As long as you feed the dogs separately, keep the puppy in a pen whenever you have to leave the two alone together, and make certain that the older dog is not given any cause for jealousy, all should be well. Within a few days, the two will have become inseparable pals.

If the scheme does not work out, however, you will have to spend extended periods of time with the dogs to allow them to get to know one another in a more gradual way. Do not allow any growling, and praise lavishly every sign of friendly behaviour. Never leave them alone together, but take every opportunity of having them in the same room whenever you are there to supervise matters. It is very rare for dogs to be totally incompatible; indeed, most older dogs seem to receive a new lease of life when a puppy is introduced to the family circle.

Introducing a puppy or older dog to a family cat can be very tricky, for the dog's first instinct is to rush forward and try to sniff the cat all over. A cat will resent this and may respond by clawing at the dog's nose. It is important to let the cat know that the dog is to be a permanent member of the family, and to provide a high shelf so that it can

escape the exuberant attentions of the newcomer. Some cats refuse to accept dogs into the household, while others welcome them and are soon sleeping happily in the same basket. Patience on the part of the owner is very important, and jealousy between the animals must be avoided at all costs.

House-training the puppy

House-training can be a simple task with some puppies, but with others it can be a long and frustrating affair. It is the first and possibly the most important set of lessons that your puppy will learn and it must be taught with care and understanding. A great deal of patience is required; the puppy must be praised warmly whenever it performs in a satisfactory manner, but it must not be unduly chastised when it makes mistakes. The puppy's built-in behaviour patterns will help with all aspects of training so that, although it has little control over its bodily functions until it is 12 weeks old, it will always try to move away from its bed before emptying itself. If you watch your puppy carefully you will see that after it wakes from a deep sleep it will start to play, then after 5 or 10 minutes it circles backwards before defecating. Play resumes for 15 or 20 minutes more, and is followed by an hour's sleep before the cycle starts again. Defecation also occurs about five minutes after each meal. It is not difficult, therefore, to guess when the puppy needs to be taken into the garden.

Many people train their pups to empty themselves on newspaper at first, and once this is successful transfer the site to the garden. Although this might be necessary in very wet weather or if the puppy is as young as six weeks, it makes the overall training more complex. It is really better to start as you mean to go on, right from the moment you acquire your little dog.

The responsible dog owner will realise the importance of hygiene in all aspects of canine care. Flat-dwellers who walk their dogs in the streets and parks should always carry a plastic bag and small scoop for the collection of their pet's droppings. Taken home, these can be wrapped in newspaper and placed in the dustbin or incinerator. Those who have suitable gardens should prepare a section, preferably screened, for use by the dog. It is unsatisfactory to allow your dog to soil random areas of the lawn and flowerbeds; furthermore, the urine of the female dog soon patterns grassed areas with round brown patches. The chosen area of garden should be well drained and spread with a fairly thick layer of coarse sand ballast, gravel, or ashes topped by dry garden peat. Urine will filter through the top layers and droppings will soon dry out, when they can be removed and disposed of. A supply of fresh peat is useful for raking over the area from time to time.

During house-training the young puppy must be lifted and put on this chosen spot whenever you think it is likely to produce results. Remember to choose the most favourable times, five minutes after feeding or after the start of play. Say 'Be good!' or 'Hurry up!' and repeat it in a friendly but brisk tone. When your timing produces a successful result, be lavish in your praise of the puppy and rub its ears or pat its chest. Suitable praise words include 'Very good!', 'Good boy!' or 'Good girl!', as the case may be, with the emphasis always given to the first word. Only after several successes should you begin to punish errors; even then you must be satisfied that they are the fault of the puppy and not the consequence of your lack of attention.

On no account must you slap or smack a puppy at this stage; neither must you indulge in the old-fashioned and barbaric practice of rubbing the pup's nose in its puddles or messes. Any punishment must be given within 30 seconds of the misdeed, otherwise the puppy will not relate the action to the deed. The most effective punishment that you can give closely resembles the sort that would be given by the puppy's mother. A gruff 'No!' sounds very like a bitch's remonstrative growl and is quickly understood. Taking hold of the loose skin at the scruff of the puppy's neck and giving it a shake also works well and simulates canine behaviour, for a bitch will often shake her puppies in this way if they misbehave.

Early failures in house-training are generally due to lack of surveillance. Dogs rarely bark to ask to go out but they do indicate their needs in many ways. During house-training you must be constantly attentive to the pup's needs.

It is a good idea to confine the young puppy to a pen at night. The floor within can be protected with a thick layer of newspaper; the puppy's bed should be placed inside the pen along with a non-spill bowl of water. Ensure that the pup is given the opportunity to use its garden patch before being settled for the night.

Bladder control at night is slow to develop, so you should rise early in the morning and take the puppy outside at the first opportunity. The little dog will urinate as soon as it wakens, a routine that is quickly established. It will help to reinforce a successful training pattern. If your puppy persistently defecates at night, alter the feeding time by providing the last meal much earlier. This will give the puppy a chance to empty itself before bedtime. Replacing a milk and cereal feed with a smaller meat feed, or vice versa, sometimes helps, but as each puppy is different it is really a matter of trial and error with your own dog.

The kitchen with its washable floor is generally chosen as a young dog's first base. Any accidents should be wiped away with absorbent kitchen paper, the area washed with a mild solution of domestic bleach, then dried with more kitchen paper to prevent the puppy's pads from coming in contact with the chemical. Strong-smelling disinfectants could contain ingredients that are harmful to the young dog's health, but bleach is non-toxic and effectively kills all germs.

The young puppy will be quite happy if it is confined to its playpen for short periods during the day, and through the night. Newspapers take care of any accidents and fresh drinking water must be provided.

Should your puppy wet or soil a carpet waste no time in cleaning up, then spray the area with a little soda water. This helps to neutralise the acid content of the wastes and prevents staining.

House manners

Acceptable house manners are much easier to teach than bowel and bladder control. Begin by showing the puppy those areas of the house where it is allowed to go, and make sure it knows the parts that are out of bounds. It is not a good idea to allow your puppy to sleep on your bed or in your bedroom; it may not be healthy for you and it is certainly unhealthy for your puppy. Unless you intend to allow your adult dog to climb on all the armchairs, remove the puppy with a firm 'No!' every time it climbs up. Never relax in this type of training, for every time your word of command is ignored will serve to encourage the dog into further disobedience. Never feed scraps from the table, no matter how appealingly your pup looks at you. Such spoiling leads to even worse habits than begging for scraps, such as stealing or pawing at the knees of guests at lunch or teatime, for example.

A useful early lesson is to teach your puppy to go into its bed or basket on command. This is achieved by pointing a finger and saying either 'Go to your basket!' or 'Get in your bed!' in a firm and commanding tone. Your voice must not sound angry or else the puppy will think that this is a form of punish-

Above *Every dog should have its own special box, bed, or basket to which it may retire to rest, sleep, or be alone.*

Below *Beds that are made of moulded, heavyweight plastic are fairly resistant to chewing, comfortable, light in weight, and easy to wash and disinfect.*

ment. Put it gently in the bed, repeating the command, and reward with much praise if it stays there. Last thing at night the reward can take the form of a small biscuit or a favourite chewy toy with which it can settle down. The pup's bed should be its haven; it should enjoy going into it when told to do so. This training also has a safety aspect and the pup can be given the command as a distraction. When chasing a bee or wasp, for example, its instant obedience to the command could prevent it from being stung.

Shut the puppy alone in a room for short periods so it learns never to object vocally to being left. Gradually lengthen the periods. If the puppy has its bed and toys handy it will happily accept its temporary isolation.

Collars and leads

A puppy can be taught to wear a collar from a very early age. The first collar can be of a cheap quality and must be very light in weight. It should be buckled around the neck tightly enough to stay on when the puppy lowers its head but loosely enough for you to be able to insert two fingers between collar and neck. The collar must be checked at least every week; it is surprising how quickly puppies grow, and a tight collar can be dangerous. The puppy will soon accept its collar, and it may be left on all day if you wish. It is best to take it off at night, however, to prevent the puppy's neck from becoming marked.

The law in Great Britain requires every dog to bear its owner's name and address. To meet this requirement an engraved disc should be attached to the puppy's collar by means of a small split ring; it can then be transferred to each successive collar as the pup grows. Never add the dog's own name to the disc, as this could help anyone who tried to entice your dog away.

It is not necessary to lead-walk a young puppy, which gets all the exercise it needs by romping and playing in the house and garden. Indeed, long tiring walks can cause physical damage in the young dog. Nevertheless, you may begin lead training the puppy if you wish. Clip a light lead to the collar and allow the puppy to pull it around. After a few days hold the end of the lead and encourage the puppy to follow you. Always keep the puppy on your left-hand side; this will help with heelwork training later on. Praise the little dog when it walks eagerly alongside you. Never drag the puppy along by its lead, nor use it to tie him up or to smack him. The sight of the lead should fill a dog with excitement and anticipation of a training session or a walk; it should not be regarded as an instrument of punishment.

Never put a check chain or slip collar on a very young puppy. Such a collar could choke the little animal and the terrifying experience could make the puppy head-shy for many months afterwards.

When the puppy approaches six months of age serious training can begin. It is important to select the correct collars, leads, and other equipment according to the dog's size and breed. Short-necked and toy breeds often feel more comfortable wearing harnesses rather than collars, but harnesses are not recommended for a boisterous young puppy because continued pulling and romping could damage the animal's shoulders and forelegs. Rolled leather collars are comfortable to wear and are easy to keep in good condition. They need a weekly wash followed by the application of saddle soap, worked well in and then polished off and allowed to dry before the collar is replaced on the dog.

Large, strong, or wilful breeds may need fitting with a check or slip collar made of leather or chain links. If chain is used, bear in mind that the large curb links which twist to lie flat are the most comfortable. Narrow chains look very elegant but hurt the dog unduly, cutting into the neck whenever a corrective jerk is given on the lead. To find the correct length of chain collar required, measure around your dog's neck midway between its head and shoulders and add 50 mm (2 in) to the measurement; this is the length of chain your dog will need. Use the check collar only during training sessions, and remember to remove the dog's normal collar and disc beforehand. It is difficult to use the check collar correctly if it is impeded by the normal one. Always remove it after training as a check collar can be dangerous if left on an unsupervised dog. Your pet will soon understand that the training collar means lesson-time; and if the sessions are as enjoyable as they should be, it will show keen excitement when the check collar is produced.

An extra long training lead made of narrow leather is ideal for all but the smallest breed of puppy. It gives extra scope during early lessons, letting you work at a distance from the pup. Many leads have spring-clip attachments which can be dangerous. These clips can get caught in the fur, or snap shut on lips, ear flaps, and paws, causing pain and distress; sometimes they have to be removed by the veterinary surgeon. The best leads have clips which open and close with a sliding metal button. These are completely safe in use and are kept in good working order by applying one drop of fine machine oil to the sliding part whenever the lead is washed and cleaned.

Some owners delight in dressing-up their dogs and there are many designs available in both collars and leads. Heavily studded collars are quite unsuitable for a young dog. Others, in brightly coloured leather, are inclined to shed their dye if they get wet, tinting the dog's neck and sometimes giving rise to allergic reactions that cause irritation and distress. By visiting dog shows and training classes you will soon discover the sort of equipment knowledgeable dog handlers prefer to use.

Small dogs need long, light leads; short but strong dogs need long, tough leads; and large dogs need short but strong leads.

The finely plaited leather collar is ideal for breeds with long, soft coats.

Collars of this shape are suitable for narrow-headed dogs such as the Whippet.

Softly rolled and stitched leather collars are kind in wear to most dog breeds.

The check chain is a training aid and should be forged from large curb links.

Left *A leather collar is correctly fitted if you can comfortably insert two fingers between it and the back of the dog's neck.*

Right *By law a dog must wear a disc or tag that bears its owner's name and address.*

Caring for Your Dog

Feeding

Most dog-breeders and kennel owners have their own favoured diets for keeping their animals in tip-top condition. When you buy your first puppy you will be given a diet sheet by the breeder, and it is best to stick rigidly to this for the first few weeks. Later on, however, you can offer the puppy different types of meat or biscuit meal and change the times of feeding to fit in with your own way of life. Each dog requires a different amount of food. The weight of food given daily depends not only on the breed and size of the dog, but also on the amount of exercise it takes and whether or not it is breeding.

In the wild, dogs eat other animals and consume the whole carcase. A wild dog gorges itself after a kill, and may go for forty-eight hours before feeding again. Breeding and domestication do not seem to have had any marked effect on the dog's digestive functions, so it is logical to feed domestic dogs on meat and plenty of roughage.

Feeding a puppy is quite straightforward. From weaning until four months it will need four meals daily, two of meat and biscuit and two of milk and cereal. The biscuit should be a pure wheatmeal of good quality; the meat can be fresh mince or a canned meat specially prepared for puppies. You can feed cow's milk, goat's milk, or correctly diluted evaporated milk to your puppy. The milk may be thickened by adding fine cereal of the sort made for human babies. Alternate the two types of meal by giving a milky feed first thing in the morning, a meat feed at midday, another milky one at tea-time and the second meat meal for supper. When fresh meat is given rather than the specially formulated canned puppy meat you must add vitamins A and D to the diet; and large breeds need additional calcium, often given in the form of sterilised bone meal.

When the puppy reaches four months the first of the milk feeds can be discontinued and the times of the other three meals brought forward slightly, the quantities being increased a little if necessary. You can soon gauge whether or not your puppy is getting the right amount of food. If it is having too little it will look thin, with its ribs showing under the skin. If it is having too much it will be lethargic, with thickening around the waist and neck. At six months reduce the number of meals a day to two, both of meat and meal; from nine months, just one main meal a day is sufficient.

The canned varieties of manufactured dog food are of two types: those that are all meat and those that are a combination of meat and cereal. Cooked meats like brawn are available as well as sachets of semi-moist pellets which contain all the nutritional needs of the dog if fed with plenty of water. There are complete dry diets, too, manufactured in the form of hard pellets and specially formulated to provide the dog with all essential nutrients when given with water. In terms of calorific values, a growing puppy requires about 220 kcal (kilocalories) per kg (kilogram) of bodyweight each day, whereas an older dog taking little exercise would require only 55 kcal/kg per day. The leading brands of canned dog meat each contain an average of 300 kcal per 376 g (13¼ oz) can; pure wheatmeal, weighed dry, contains 3550 kcal/kg. Whole cow's milk has about 650 kcal/litre (370 kcal/pint).

Food should be served at room temperature; if it is given straight from the refrigerator it could cause gastric upsets. Always put the food in a clean bowl of the right size and shape for the breed. A healthy dog will eat its food very quickly and lick the bowl clean. If it leaves some food, you should remove what is unwanted and so prevent the dog from becoming a finicky feeder. Never leave a dish containing uneaten food on the floor; it will only attract flies and can lead to infection and disease. Feed your dog at regular times and do not give titbits between meals. It is important that the dog has access to fresh, clean drinking water at all times; again be sure to choose the right shape of dish for your dog and wash it out every morning before refilling it. Always keep the water bowl in the same place.

Buy some extra hard biscuits for your young dog and give it one each night when you tell it to go to bed. Chewing these biscuits prevents the boredom which often leads to destructive behaviour at night; the biscuit also helps to remove traces of tartar from the teeth. A marrow bone is excellent for your dog, either raw or cooked. Other

Pages 20–21 A boy and his dog – the best of friends. Rough collies make loyal family dogs but, like other long-haired breeds, need thorough grooming.

Left and below *This tall bowl is made especially for long-eared dogs and prevents the ears from becoming soiled. Young puppies need calcium and this is provided by giving milk with cereal twice daily.*

Dark oblong dish: feeding dish with meat and meal

Light oblong dish: bowl of crunchy dog biscuits

Tall bowl: Spaniel bowl, with cereal

Two-compartment bowl: divided dish with (left) semi-moist dog-diet and (right) complete dehydrated dog-diet

bones, however, may splinter and cause physical damage if swallowed.

If you give your dog a well-balanced diet it will not need extra vitamin pills and tonics. You may find, however, that a little margarine or vegetable oil in its food will help counteract a dull or scurfy coat at moulting time, and the occasional egg or dish of liver or fish will benefit the dog's general health.

Vaccinations

Dogs should always be protected by vaccination against the major canine diseases. Unvaccinated dogs may easily become infected when using parks and playgrounds, staying in boarding kennels, or participating in dog shows, and they are, in fact, always at risk in any areas inhabited by other dogs. Puppies are particularly susceptible to infectious diseases and should have a systematic programme of injections.

Distemper and its close ally hardpad, is a very common and often fatal virus disease. Even a dog lucky enough to recover from an attack of distemper may be left with permanent damage to its nervous system. A puppy which contracts distemper stops eating, and

Puppies should be fed individually, so that each receives the correct amount. Here a dominant puppy tries to take the best portion from its littermate's bowl before it has finished its own portion.

its nose and eyes discharge. It coughs and suffers acutely from both sickness and diarrhoea in the second stage of the disease, when the discharges become purulent and the animal begins to dehydrate rapidly. Secondary infections occur in this stage and may cause death. Sometimes, after an apparent recovery, a dog will show the third-stage symptoms of distemper as a result of extensive damage to the nervous system. These distressing signs include poor co-ordination, fits, paralysis, and coma, finally leading to death. In some cases the typical rigid appearance of the paw pads indicates hardpad; in other dogs whole groups of muscles may be seen to twitch uncontrollably.

Canine viral hepatitis is a disease of dogs which particularly affects the liver. It attacks very quickly. The affected animal stops eating, runs a very high temperature, and drinks copious quantities of water. It shows severe conjunctivitis, may vomit from time to time, and reacts strongly if touched anywhere near the lower ribs because of its painfully enlarged liver. In some cases its skin may look very jaundiced. Good veterinary care and careful home nursing enable the large majority of dogs to recover. Some sufferers additionally develop a phenomenon known as blue eye, in which the cornea becomes blue in colour. This condition generally clears after a few days, but sometimes it will persist longer.

Leptospirosis is caused in the dog by either of two closely related bacteria which can also affect man, so it is particularly important to control this disease in the canine population. The liver or kidneys may be affected and the disease is severe and painful, usually ending in death. Affected dogs refuse to eat, but drink lots of water. They dehydrate rapidly through persistent vomiting and resent being touched anywhere near their abdominal organs.

Parvo disease is caused in dogs by a specific canine parvovirus and is highly infectious. It affects the heart muscle in very young puppies, which quickly succumb and die, usually within three days of the onset of the illness. Infected older puppies and adult dogs become suddenly ill with severe enteritis and they dehydrate rapidly. Prompt and expert care is needed to save their lives.

Fortunately, all these serious diseases can be prevented in the dog by vaccination. Bitches which have high antibody levels as a result of regular vaccinations, pass on protection to their puppies through their milk supply. Each puppy varies in the length of time it retains these maternal antibodies within its own system, however, and because of this many breeders prefer to immunise each puppy by injection at an early stage in its life.

A special treatment is available in which a living measles vaccine protects the pup against distemper, and two other vaccines immunise against hepatitis and the two forms of leptospirosis.

Giving liquid medicines

To administer liquid medicines, have the dog sitting comfortably at your side. Pull out the lip while the jaws remain closed: this forms a natural funnel down which the measured dose may be poured from a plastic spoon and seen to be swallowed.

This primary course should be given at six weeks; it can then be reinforced by a further injection against the four diseases when the puppy is between 12 and 14 weeks old.

Although parvo disease was not positively identified until 1978, an effective vaccine for it was quickly produced. Given to the bitch before mating or during pregnancy, it protects her puppies by passing antibodies to them in her milk. A temporary dose of the same vaccine can be given to the litter at weaning and a permanent dose administered once the little dogs reach 12 weeks of age. As each puppy may have slightly different vaccination requirements, depending on the programme begun by its breeder, it is imperative that you discuss the phasing of your pet's injections with your veterinary surgeon. A timetable of vaccinations is then drawn up, probably combined with routine worming. This programme should be precisely followed.

Giving medicines

Medicines prescribed for your dog that are to be given by mouth should never be mixed with food. The correct dosage is important, but your dog may be too ill to eat its meal or it may detect the substance in the food and decide to leave it untouched. With all but the most vicious of dogs, however, giving pills and liquid medicines is a fairly simple matter.

Liquid medicines are usually prescribed in 5 ml (one teaspoon) doses. They can be given by means of the plastic measuring spoon that is often provided with the medicine, or with a plastic syringe that you can get from the veterinary surgeon. Measure the dose and sit the dog by your side. Hold its jaws closed, tilt the head well back, then pull out the flap of the lip on one side of the mouth. This forms a natural funnel down which the liquid can be poured. Keep holding the dog's head up and do not release it until you have seen it swallow. Gentle rubbing of the throat will help the process along.

Medication supplied in powder form should never be poured into the dog's mouth because the fine particles can cause choking. Instead, mix powders with honey or margarine and smear the resulting paste on the dog's tongue with a plastic palate knife or the handle of a spoon. Dogs generally enjoy such a dose and eagerly accept the next one.

Giving pills and tablets

Sit the dog comfortably at your side, then place your hand over the muzzle, pressing the lips against the animal's teeth. Holding the pill in your other hand, use a finger to open the dog's mouth, then pop the pill or tablet right at the back of the throat. Rub the dog's throat until it swallows.

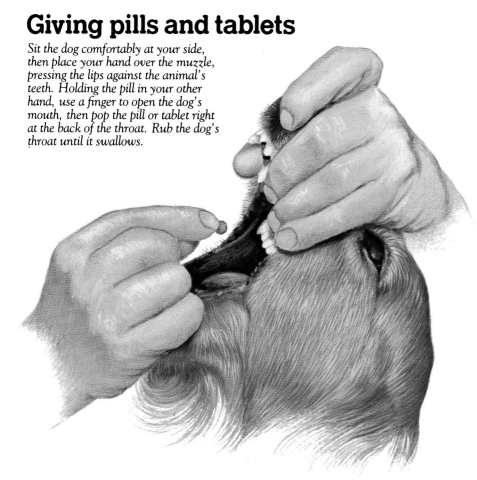

The technique for giving tablets, pills, and capsules requires a little practice. Sit your dog in front of you so that it looks towards your right. Place your left hand over its muzzle, just in front of the eyes, and gently press its lips inwards onto the teeth. With your right hand, open the mouth by pressing the front of the lower jaw downwards; simultaneously, slightly close your left hand so that the dog's lips cover its teeth. This effectively prevents the dog from closing its mouth, but it is important not to hold the mouth so tightly that your pet is hurt, struggles, or whines. Take the pill or tablet in your right hand and place it at the back of the dog's tongue. Allow the mouth to shut, hold the jaws closed and the nose pointing upwards, and use the right hand to rub the dog's throat until you see it swallow. Be sure to praise your dog when the dose is taken. These are instructions for the right-handed owner; if you are left-handed, merely reverse them.

Importance of worming

The dog can be host to two main groups of parasitic worms, roundworms and tapeworms. Dosing against worm infest-ation is an extremely important and often underrated aspect of dog care, and it should be carried out under veterinary supervision if it is to be wholly effective. Tablets are generally prescribed, the dose depending on the animal's weight. Patent medicines have to err on the side of safety and may not be strong enough or contain the correct ingredients to deal efficiently with the worms infesting your dog. There is a danger, too, of wrongly diagnosing an ailing dog's condition as being due to worms. Most of the drugs used for treating worms can produce side-effects which may prove fatal to a sick dog, so correct diagnosis by the veterinary surgeon is essential.

Most common of the canine parasites is the roundworm, the larvae of which infect the puppy while it is still inside the bitch's womb. Within three days of birth the worms reach the puppy's intestine, where they grow and mature by the ninth day, producing eggs of their own by the time the puppy is two months old. The infective eggs pass out in the puppy's faeces and are taken up by another host. If a puppy under three weeks of age picks up and swallows the eggs, the larvae will hatch in the intestines before migrating through the bowel wall and into the liver. They are then carried through the bloodstream to the lungs, producing in the puppy a dry cough. Coughing raises the worms into the mouth and they are swallowed; they return to the intestine where they can grow into mature adults, starting the cycle all over again. If the original infective eggs are swallowed by a puppy over three weeks of age, the larvae hatch in the intestine and then pass into various body tissues where they remain dormant.

A puppy heavily infested with roundworms will be in poor general condition and may have a swollen belly. It may be very constipated or else have diarrhoea, and during the migration of the worms through the lungs it could have breathing problems or a dry cough.

The roundworm eggs are very sticky and extremely small. In playing with an infected puppy, a small child can easily and unknowingly contaminate its fingers and transfer the eggs to its mouth. As roundworms can cause unpleasant symptoms in humans it is very important to ensure that routine hygienic measures are taken with all young puppies. The animals should have their own dishes and bowls, washed separately from those of the human family; hands should be carefully washed after playing with or handling young puppies; no dog of any age should be allowed to lick a human face; and faeces should be carefully cleaned up and disposed of. Such routine care combined with systematic worming treatment should eradicate any roundworm problems in your puppy.

The tapeworm causes fewer problems in the dog. It is not passed from dog to dog but develops in a secondary or intermediate host. The host of the common tapeworm of the dog, Dipylidium caninum, is the dog flea. If a dog eats the host animal, the tapeworm attaches itself by its head to the wall of the intestines of the dog and begins to grow. As each segment develops to maturity and ripens with eggs, it breaks away from the rest of the worm and passes out in the dog's faeces to begin a new cycle in its specific host. Special worming tablets are required to rid the dog of tapeworm. Re-infestation can be prevented by keeping the animal free from fleas.

The presence of a tapeworm in the dog rarely seems to cause any health problems. The first signs of infestation are noticed when ripe segments, looking rather like white cucumber seeds, are noticed around the dog's anus.

Other worms are fairly rare in the

dog, but if you are concerned by an unexplained loss of condition, a ravenous appetite, or a staring coat, contact your veterinary surgeon. He may ask you to bring a sample of your pet's faeces in a clean jar or plastic bag for microscopic analysis. Any worms or eggs present will be identified and then eradicated by correct treatment.

Ear drops

The dog's ear is a delicate organ and nothing should be put into the ear canal unless it has been prescribed by the veterinary surgeon. Patent canker powders are often puffed or poured into a dog's ears by its owner in the mistaken belief that they will do some good. Instead, the particles merely clog together in the ear and cause the dog intense irritation and misery, and veterinary treatment will eventually be needed to syringe and clean out the ear canal. Veterinary ear drops, however, are specially formulated and individually prescribed, and the veterinary surgeon will demonstrate how they should be administered.

If your dog has ear mites, it is very important to use the drops at the correct, specified intervals, in order to kill the parasites, which are vulnerable to treatment only at certain times in their life cycle.

Eye ointments

Dogs suffer from inflamed and sore eyes for a variety of reasons, but two main causes are dusty bedding and hanging the head out of the window of a moving car. The dog's eyes are very delicate and must be handled carefully. Their normal healthy appearance is bright and clear, but if the whites look bloodshot or there is a discharge, clean each eye with a separate piece of cotton wool dipped in saline solution or a mild eyewash made for human use. Saline solution is made by dissolving one level tablespoonful of common salt in one pint of boiling water, allowing it to cool, and storing it in a spotlessly clean, sealed bottle.

Persistent eye trouble must receive veterinary attention. Antibiotic treatment may be given by injection and this might need to be supplemented by the application at home of specially formulated ointment. It is very important to apply the ointment exactly as shown by your veterinarian and over the full length of time. Even if the eyes appear to have got better, always continue the treatment until it has been completed: the trouble may only be masked, and could return.

Grooming

Daily grooming is an essential part of dog care and the routine should be established from the first day that you acquire your puppy or adult dog. Grooming removes old dead hair and prevents the formation of felting or matting in long-coated breeds. It stimulates the blood supply to the skin, and this in turn improves the condition of the coat, giving a healthier appearance to the dog. Correct grooming can also improve muscle tone in the dog's back and limbs and leads to a general sense of well-being. If you have little time to spare you should choose a short-coated dog, although even the most glamorous of hounds or those dogs with very profuse pelts can be kept in trim with a daily 10-minute grooming session.

Most dogs enjoy grooming, which simulates the sort of social nibbling behaviour indulged in by their wild ancestors. If you are careful not to pull or tug at tangles, and do not strike any sensitive areas, the act of grooming can

Grooming equipment

A double-sided wire/bristle brush

Wire rake (for teasing out mats)

Double-sided comb (coarse side for long thick hair, finer side for shorter, closer hair)

Fine metal comb (for fine, medium-length hair)

Short blunt-nosed scissors (for trimming over-long hair and tangles)

Body brush (for smooth-coated dogs)

Rubber grooming glove (for removing dead hair)

Grooming powder (for cleaning the coat)

reinforce your dog's affection for and trust in you.

Each type of coat requires its own set of grooming equipment. It is best to seek advice from the outset in order to avoid buying expensive brushes and combs that turn out to be unsuitable. Pet shop staff can be knowledgeable, and those who run accessory stalls at dog shows are usually experts in their field. The best person of all, however, will be the breeder of your puppy. He will be able to advise you on the right equipment and will probably be pleased to show you how it should be used.

Pure-bristle hairbrushes are needed for toy dogs and some of the smooth-coated breeds. Most types of dog require a good quality steel comb. Cheap combs are a false economy as the nickel plating soon wears through and peels off. Good combs have rounded ends to the teeth so that they are not sharp enough to scratch the dog's skin. Choose a comb with correctly spaced teeth for your dog's coat type. Remember that the longer and thicker the coat, the wider the teeth should be spaced. Short satin-like coats are best rubbed down with a grooming mitten, and for short hard coats you can buy an excellent glove.

Generally speaking, the long-coated dogs need the most attention. A good wire brush is the best tool for separating the hairs. It should be of very good quality and have wire teeth that are neither too harsh nor too soft and are firmly set into a wooden base with a comfortable handle. The wire brush must always be used gently and with care, so that the teeth do not scratch the animal's skin.

In brushing out the long-coated varieties it is best to have the dog standing comfortably and relaxed on a bench or table. This is for your benefit rather than the dog's, for it will take some time to go right through the coat, and it can be a back-breaking job if you have to bend down to do it. If the dog is inclined to be restless, tie it up with a fairly short chain on its collar and talk soothingly to it throughout the grooming. Learning to stand still for grooming is an important feature of the dog's training and should be taught as thoroughly as any other part of the training programme.

Start at the rear end with one of the hind legs. Lift the long outer hair up and use the wire brush to go through all the undercoat of the thigh and down the lower leg. Brush carefully down the inner side of the thigh where the skin may be sensitive, then groom the top coat smoothly back into place. Repeat

this procedure for the other hind leg, then thoroughly groom the rump and down the entire length of the tail. Brush out the front legs next, again lifting the top coat and grooming the undercoat first.

Some dogs object strongly to being groomed underneath; this is usually because they have not been properly taught to accept it from puppyhood. If you buy an adult long-coated breed which proves almost impossible to groom, have the underneath hair professionally clipped away, perhaps under a general anaesthetic given by the veterinary surgeon. You can then retrain the dog to accept grooming as the

Grooming improves the appearance of a dog. Here a wire-toothed brush is used to remove loose undercoat from a Labrador. Such a dog benefits most from use of a bristle brush followed by a hound glove.

hair grows through slowly and before it has the chance to become tangled and cause the animal pain. Pay particular care to the area between the forelimbs and along the belly; bear in mind that these parts can be ticklish and tender, and it will be necessary to tease out any small tangles or knots. In this area the hair can be extremely soft and fine, and easily mats together. Grass seeds and prickles get caught up in this soft hair

Grooming a long-coated dog

1 *The top coat is lifted forward so that the undercoat may be thoroughly brushed.*

2 *The hind legs are dealt with first of all and groomed down to the pads.*

3 *The dog may be sensitive in this area and any knots should be teased out.*

4 *The tail must be treated gently, paying extra attention to the fine feathering.*

5 *In using the wire brush, care must be taken to avoid scratching the dog's skin.*

6 *After dealing with the undercoat, each layer of top coat is smoothed into place.*

7 *The brush is then used down the throat and between the forelegs.*

8 *The bristle brush is used to groom the long, fine hair behind the dog's ears.*

9 *Careful combings of all soft areas can help to prevent the formation of mats.*

10 *A fine-toothed comb removes grit, dirt, and dust from the hair between the toes.*

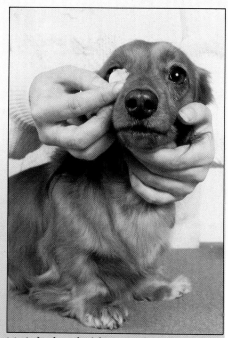

11 *A fresh pad of dampened cotton wool is used carefully to clean each eye.*

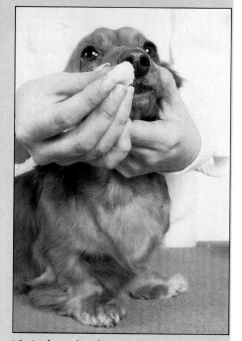

12 *And another dampened pad is used to remove any discharge from the nostrils.*

and cause tangles which may have to be clipped out with blunt-nosed scissors if they are not promptly removed by brushing.

Groom the body hair from the shoulders back over the ribs to the hips. Brush down the neck and chest, then deal with any long hair on the face and the ears if they have long furnishings. After you have gone all over the dog with the wire brush and are certain that no areas have been missed, use a metal comb to deal with any feathering or extra long hair around the head, ears, legs or tail.

Follow the same general pattern for grooming short-coated breeds, starting at the hind legs, progressing to the body and finishing with the head. Most dogs benefit from a final polish with a soft, clean chamois-leather or a silk or velvet pad to bring up a gloss on the coat. White legs and feet can be rubbed with powdered chalk to remove any trace of discoloration, and grooming powder will help to keep the hair from matting too quickly in fine, soft coats.

The dog's feet need careful attention, especially if there is long hair between the toes. All sorts of things can get caught here, like small stones or seeds which embed themselves into the soft skin and cause intense irritation. Feel between the toes with your fingers, then use a small comb to separate the hairs. The pads can receive a lot of punishment, especially when the animal takes a type of exercise that differs from what it is accustomed to. A dog which normally exercises on grass but has a day out involving lots of roadwork like going with its owner on a sponsored walk may damage its pads quite severely. A day at the beach may be an unusual and enjoyable experience for the dog but could possibly harm its feet. Take time during the daily grooming to examine the pads. Apply a little vegetable oil and work it well into the skin if they look dry or cracked, and pack in some antiseptic ointment if they are bruised or lacerated.

Finish the grooming procedure by cleaning the dog's eyes and nostrils. Use a fresh piece of damp cotton wool to wipe out each eye and another piece for the nostrils. If the nose is inclined to dry up or become caked with dirt, try softening it with petroleum jelly rubbed well into the skin. The ears must be kept clean at all times. Use dry cotton buds to wipe away accumulated dust and wax from the complicated folds inside the ear flaps. Never use these buds to poke around within the ear, however. If you do so you may easily damage the ear's delicate structures.

Stripping and trimming

Some breeds require specialist trimming to keep their coats manageable, and this should be taken into account when you are considering the sort of dog to buy. A few breeds can be lightly trimmed to make their coats more manageable: the Cocker Spaniel, for example, may have the feathering on its legs shortened and the long hair between the toes clipped out. Most of the terriers need stripping at regular intervals, and this entails the expert hand-plucking of surplus hair from the coat. Clipping terriers ruins the typical weatherproof structure of their coat. Poodles are generally clipped professionally into classic designs, but it is possible for owners to keep their dogs shaped into simple trims with hand clippers and hairdressing scissors.

Nails

If your dog is regularly exercised on hard surfaces its nails are unlikely to need any attention for they will naturally wear down to the correct length. The nails of dogs confined to grassy areas, or walked only in the park, can grow excessively long, however, and must be clipped back to enable the animal to walk properly. Always use guillotine-type nail clippers to cut your dog's nails, and ask your veterinary surgeon to show you how to use them correctly. Dogs dislike having their nails cut at any time so it is doubly important for you to know the correct point at which the nail should be shortened to avoid cutting the sensitive quick. If you cut too close to the quick you will hurt your dog; and if the nail is cut too short it will bleed profusely.

Dewclaws

The dewclaws on the forelimbs of most breeds are often removed when the puppies are three or four days old, although veterinary surgeons are divided as to whether this is a good or bad thing. If the front dewclaws have been left on your dog, keep an eye on them and clip them back periodically; they tend to grow very long if unchecked.

Many dogs are born without dewclaws on their hindlimbs. When dewclaws are present, however, they are in vestigial form with no bony attachment to the foot; there are no problems in removing them from the very young pup. Left on, such claws tend to grow long and catch in all manner of objects, often tearing away from the limb and bleeding profusely. It is best to have these claws removed surgically if they regularly cause trouble.

Anal sacs and glands

The dog has a pair of sacs which lie inside the body cavity just below and on either side of its anus. These sacs store a distinctively and powerfully pungent grey-brown fluid produced by the two anal glands which surround them. A small duct leads from each sac to the opening of the anus. Each time the dog defecates, a little of the fluid passes up the tube and is smeared on the stool, giving it its characteristic doggy odour. This scent is important in the wild dog, acting as a territorial marking agent.

The anal sacs sometimes present problems in the domestic dog, becoming impacted and failing to drain adequately. An affected dog may drag its seat across the ground in an attempt to relieve the irritation, or it will try to bite the area. If neglected the anal sacs will become infected and antibiotic treatment will be required. The veterinary surgeon can empty the sacs manually whenever necessary and will show you how to do this yourself if you wish.

To empty the sacs, put on rubber gloves and take a large piece of cotton wool in one hand. Hold the dog by the root of its tail with the other hand, place the cotton wool over the region of the anal sacs and press inwards and upwards with your thumb and forefinger. This action does not hurt the dog and the offensive matter will pass out into the cotton wool pad.

Fed a good diet and given adequate exercise, some dogs never have any trouble with their anal sacs while others seem to spend a good part of their lives going to and from the surgery. If the problem is persistent it is advisable to have the sacs and glands removed surgically, which does not seem to adversely affect the dog.

Teeth

The dog has 42 teeth consisting of 12 incisors, 4 canines, 16 premolars, 4 upper molars and 6 lower ones. Because of the great diversity in canine skull shapes, dentition can vary. In recent years, for example, Poodles have tended to have fewer incisors than previously owing to the elongation of the lower jaw which has become narrower at the front. In some breeds the incisors form a double row as a result of deformation of the jaw. When teeth do not meet correctly, or the first teeth are not properly shed, retention of trapped food particles can lead to dental disease.

Clean your dog's mouth once a week by rubbing the teeth and gums with a slice of lemon; alternatively, your veterinary surgeon will be able to recommend a suitable preparation for use as a canine toothpaste. Ensure that your dog has good strong teeth, which can be kept healthy through correct diet and very hard biscuit plus the occasional marrow bone. If you notice a build-up of tartar, have it removed by your veterinary surgeon or clean the teeth yourself. You can purchase a special scaling tool for the job. Hold it at the base of the tooth between the gum and the scale. Draw it firmly down (or up) the tooth and the scale lifts away, leaving the enamel clean once more. Some dogs have permanently stained teeth following virus infections in puppyhood and this condition cannot be rectified.

Bathing your dog

There is no need to bath your dog if it is kept clean and sweet-smelling with normal grooming. Bathing removes the coat's natural oils which act as weather-

When bathing a dog, you should wash the face first, using clean water to wipe the eyes and nostrils and to deal with any soiled areas around mouth and lips.

After thoroughly wetting the entire coat, apply a special dog shampoo, following the manufacturer's instructions and rubbing it well into the coat.

proofing agents, so that a dog which lives in the open could be detrimentally affected by too-frequent tubbings. Pet dogs which live in centrally heated homes often shed a lot of hair and may need fairly frequent baths to keep fresh, clean and tidy. Apart from removing the coat's oils, bathing is not otherwise detrimental to the dog's health if it is carried out correctly and the animal is thoroughly dried before it can catch a chill.

Some short-coated dogs may go their entire lives without ever needing a bath. Others which need regular stripping, clipping or trimming are often bathed at these times as the freshly washed coat is then easier to handle. Long-coated breeds, and those which are regularly shown, generally have quite frequent bathing sessions. Bathing a smallish, short-coated dog is comparatively easy, but bathing a large, long-coated dog may take time and a great deal of patience, especially if the animal is unco-operative.

Small breeds can be bathed in a disused baby-bath, or a large bowl; larger breeds will need the family bath tub or may be placed near a drain outlet, preferably on concrete, and

have warm water poured over them from a bucket or tub. If it is necessary to bath a dog outdoors, it must be done on a warm day. If the bath or sink is used, place a small rubber mat at the bottom to help the animal feel more secure. Every dog must be thoroughly groomed before bathing, with any matted hair being teased or clipped out. Make sure the dog has a chance to relieve itself before you begin.

A hand spray is useful for wetting the coat and giving the final rinse; alternatively, you can use a jug or large sponge for the purpose. A large plastic apron or a flimsy plastic raincoat put on the wrong way round will help to keep you dry. Remove everything from the bathing area before you begin in case the dog slips through your wet hands, and firmly shut the door.

Take off the dog's collar and sit the animal in the bowl or tub. Wash its face carefully and wipe out the ears; put a smear of Vaseline along the eyelids and plug the ears with non-absorbent cotton wool, also smeared with Vaseline. Thoroughly wet the coat from the neck downwards then apply the dog shampoo, following the manufacturer's directions, and work up a lather. Wash

the dog's coat thoroughly and pay particular attention to the underparts, around the tail and between the toes. Use fresh water to rinse every trace of shampoo from the coat. Take care to keep the shampoo and rinsing water out of the dog's eyes, nose and ears and use tepid water only throughout the bathing process.

When the dog is rinsed, squeeze as much of the surplus water as possible out of the coat and down the legs, envelop him in a large towel and place him on the floor. Encourage him to give a really good shake. Towel as much moisture as you can from the coat, then use a drier or another dry towel to finish the job. If you have a breed that needs regular bathing, it would be wise to invest in a drier specially made for dogs. Long straight coats should be groomed into place during drying. You will need one hand for the brush and one hand for the drier, so tie the dog up or have it held throughout this rather long and tedious process. If you do have to tie up your dog, be sure to use a metal check chain or similar collar because a leather collar that gets wet may shed dye onto the coat around the dog's neck.

Every trace of shampoo must be rinsed from the coat, using plenty of tepid water. Take care that the water does not enter the dog's ears or eyes.

Finally, dry the dog thoroughly using a rough towel, and (unless it is frightened or objects strongly) finish off with an ordinary hair dryer, set at 'cool'.

Twelve golden rules for the dog owner

1 Feed your dog at regular times, avoiding titbits between meals.

2 Provide suitable dishes for your dog's food and water, and wash these separately from those of the rest of the family.

3 Provide your dog with its own draught-proof bed.

4 Keep your dog clean and properly groomed.

5 Train your dog so that it is under control at all times.

6 Do not allow your dog to disturb neighbours by barking.

7 Never allow your dog to foul pavements, lawns, gardens, or open spaces where children play.

8 Keep your dog on its lead along or near roads or where there is farm livestock.

9 Never take your dog (unless it is a Guide Dog) into food shops.

10 Find good boarding kennels and book a place there early if you intend to take a holiday without your dog.

11 Get to know your local veterinary surgeon and arrange regular health checks and vaccinations for your dog.

12 Ensure that your dog is never responsible for producing unwanted puppies. Seek veterinary advice if necessary.

The bitch

In general the female dog comes into oestrus (or comes 'on heat', as it is popularly termed) twice a year. There can be considerable differences between individuals and breeds, however, and there is no need to panic if your own bitch comes on heat at seven, eight or ten months – just so long as she is regular. Some bitches have a heat only once a year, notably those of the Basenji breed, which originated in Central Africa. Bitches of the smaller breeds tend to have more frequent heats than those of larger varieties.

The male dog

Male puppies often go through the motions of mounting and simulated mating from the age of a few weeks, but when they go to their new homes away from their litter mates this behaviour ceases. The male dog that is bought as a pet should be kept away from sexual temptation; it is not necessary for him to have any sexual experience in the course of his life. It is a great mistake to allow such a dog to mate a bitch, as he might become disorientated and begin to wander; he might start marking out a territory in the home with his urine and become aggressive towards other male dogs. Dogs used for stud work are specially trained from the age of about 10 months and are regularly used for mating. Their life-style is unlike that of the pet dog.

Some young male dogs respond to a surge in their hormone levels between six months and one year of age, and may embarrass their owners by increased sexual behaviour. Such dogs may mount furniture, other pets, children or the legs of visitors. Every time this unacceptable behaviour occurs the dog must be distracted and given some other form of energetic play. Although you can ask your veterinary surgeon to castrate the dog, this is not always necessary; given time and patience the matter will probably right itself. Castration of the male dog is a simple operation, but it totally changes the animal's personality and some veterinary surgeons are reluctant to do it unless there is no alternative. The castrated dog is less active than the entire dog and care must be taken with his diet to ensure that he does not become overweight. He is less interested in life and may lose his instinct to guard the home.

Large breeds benefit from living outdoors; they should have warm, dry kennels, away from prevailing winds. Dogs usually become attached to their personal kennels, as this German Shepherd obviously is, and willingly go into them when told to.

The young bitch matures sexually at about six to nine months, although she may still be growing physically and mentally. The first sign of oestrus is a noticeable swelling of the vulva, which the bitch will constantly lick. This licking and cleaning indicates the onset of blood loss when the womb sheds its lining and prepares to receive fertilised eggs. Bleeding continues for about 10 days. During this time the bitch is attractive to male dogs, although she will not permit mating to take place. When taken for walks at this stage, the bitch will stop frequently to pass small amounts of urine, which serves to mark her whereabouts and advertise her impending condition to any interested suitors. From the tenth to the fourteenth day from the onset of the bleeding, the bitch is ready and willing to be mated. During this time the eggs are shed by the ovary, the discharge changes to a straw-coloured fluid and the vulva becomes very large and soft. If breeding puppies is your aim, this is the period of the heat in which mating must take place if it is to be successful. If you do not want any puppies, however, you will have to take extra care to prevent your bitch from getting out or a visiting dog from getting in.

Never underestimate the sexual drive of your pet and be sure to carefully secure all doors, gates, and windows at this critical part of the heat period. It is possible to buy patent sprays, tablets, and lotions manufactured to help mask your bitch's condition but do not rely on them completely; they are only aids, not foolproof preventives.

From the fourteenth day, the bitch will begin to lose interest in males, and the heat is usually over by the twenty-first day. Although the optimum time is midway through oestrus, mating and conception can occur up to the last day. Your vigilance must not wane

until the bitch has returned to her normal quiescent condition.

Progesterone tablets can be given to totally suppress oestrus in the bitch by inhibiting ovulation. If you find it impossible to cope and you never want puppies, you could consider having your pet spayed. The operation involves removing the womb and ovaries. A spayed bitch will not have any further heats, she cannot have unwanted puppies and will not be prone to false pregnancies in later life. She will retain her female character and continue to be a home-loving pet. She may require slightly less food than her entire counterpart, so her diet must be monitored to ensure that she does not put on excess weight. Veterinary opinion varies as to the best age for spaying. Some surgeons favour around five months, well before the first 'season', whilst others prefer to operate after the first heat has passed.

Breeding

Should you decide to breed from your bitch, have her checked over by the veterinary surgeon to make sure that she is in good physical condition and does not have any defects which might give problems during gestation, whelping, or lactation. The breeder of your bitch might be the best person to advise you about the choice of stud dog. A local dog is preferable to one that lives miles away. Bitches in season are naturally stressed, and a long tiring journey may upset her so much that she rejects the dog's advances on arrival.

Mating may be a brief encounter lasting 10 minutes or so, or a protracted affair of an hour or more. If the bitch is at the suitable stage in her heat, she will stand patiently while the dog mounts her and mating takes place. The anatomy of the dog is such that the mated pair are unable to separate immediately after mating. The dog gets down from the mating position and turns so that the pair stand back to back in the attitude known as the tie. Both dogs must be kept relaxed and calm at this time and under no circumstances should anyone try to separate them. After a while, the dogs will part naturally and both clean themselves.

The gestation period is nine weeks, but the puppies may appear a few days earlier or later than this. During those 63 days the pups slowly develop and the bitch's abdomen increases in size in order to accommodate them. There is very little change in appearance and behaviour in the first four weeks; by the fifth week, however, the mammary glands show signs of enlargement and

the bitch may have slight morning sickness. By the sixth week the abdomen is definitely larger. You should now start to give an extra meal in the middle of the day.

The pregnant bitch should have high-quality and well-balanced meals throughout the gestation period. She must be kept fit and not allowed to get fat. Your veterinary surgeon will tell you whether you should give any extra vitamin or mineral supplements. Tell him of the expected birth date in case you need to call him out. Towards the end of the pregnancy, the bitch's shape may change dramatically as the development of the puppies speeds up, and her breasts might secrete a milk-like substance. Well before the expected delivery date, prepare the whelping area. This may either be a large box, a small room or a partitioned-off corner of the kitchen. The confinement should take place in a warm dry place, free from draughts and away from too much household bustle.

Loss of appetite is one of the first signs that whelping is imminent, and the bitch may go without food for 24 hours. She will also appear very restless and may repeatedly go to the whelping box and tear at the newspaper placed there. This tearing of paper harks back to the behaviour of the wild dog, which would start to dig a deep burrow at this time in preparation for the birth. Just before the actual birth begins, the bitch's temperature will drop from 38.5°C to 38°C.

Although whelping is a natural process, you may wish to call your veterinary surgeon so that he is ready to come out to help if necessary. Most whelpings are quite normal and even the maiden bitch copes beautifully. Many novice owners are distressed by the frantic panting that the bitch often makes in the first stages of labour, but the panting subsides when whelping gets under way. Regular contractions usually produce the first puppy about an hour or so after straining begins, and the rest of the litter arrive at about 30-minute intervals. With very large litters, the bitch may tire and the last puppies will be spaced further apart.

Each puppy is born enclosed in its foetal sac, which the bitch removes by vigorous licking. This frees the youngster's head and enables it to breathe. The bitch usually cleans away the membranes and, in doing so, severs the umbilical cord. It is quite usual for her to lick up and swallow all the debris of birth, including the placentae. (In the wild, these provide the bitch with valuable nourishment while she rests

This Great Dane bitch is naturally protective of her puppies during the first weeks after their birth. Her feelings must be respected and she should be disturbed as little as possible during this period.

and recovers from the birth of her litter.) If the bitch is unable to clean and stimulate her puppies, you must do it for her. The most important thing to remember is to quickly clear the puppies' mouths and nostrils so that they can breathe. Dry the puppies with clean, rough towelling. You do not have to be in too much of a hurry to cut or break the umbilical cord.

After giving birth the bitch's instincts are to hide and protect her babies. She does not like an audience at the birth or during the first days with her litter. Take care to see that nothing happens which will cause her to be distressed or unduly disturbed.

When your bitch has produced her last puppy, she will settle down and gather them all to her. You should remove some of the soiled wet bedding and replace it with paper towelling or a blanket of the special polyester fur material specially made for such occasions. It is important that the puppies all suckle and receive the special first-milk, or colostrum, which contains the precious maternal antibodies that protect the puppies from possible disease during the first weeks of life.

The litter

Puppies are born blind and deaf but with a keen sense of smell which enables them to find the bitch's teats. They spend the first few days suckling and sleeping and are stimulated to urinate and defecate by the licking action of their mother, who keeps them and their nest scrupulously clean. Hearing gradually develops and the eyes open on the ninth or tenth day. After three weeks the puppies can see quite well and are very active, indulging in mock fights and making little sorties from the whelping box. Although the bitch will continue to feed them for the first six weeks or longer, they will accept solid food from the third week and quickly learn to lap from a shallow dish. The litter should be gradually weaned away from the bitch during the sixth, seventh, and eighth weeks to allow her milk supply to dry up naturally. From the sixth week, the bitch's attitude will have changed dramatically from that of a protective, devoted mother to one of mere tolerance. She will not be unduly worried when the puppies leave for their new homes when eight to twelve weeks old.

Basic Dog Training

Early lessons

Every dog should be trained in basic obedience. The owner who is prepared to spend a few minutes every day giving simple lessons will be repaid many times over in the enjoyment of owning a well-behaved pet.

The puppy coming into the family circle for the first time has no notion of the way in which it is expected to behave. Until this time it has had the companionship of its mother and siblings and has been able, to a large extent, to follow its own innate behaviour patterns as regards eating, drinking, playing, sleeping and excreting. Once it leaves the litter it has many lessons to learn in order to fit in with its owner's way of life.

The first lessons a puppy must learn are simple and easy to teach. First of all it must come whenever it is called, it must walk properly without pulling forward or backwards on the lead, and it must stay when told to do so without moving or whining. A puppy must learn to walk along without sniffing and examining every fence, lamp-post, or tree-trunk, and it must also be taught that there are proper times and appropriate

Pages 36–7 Road sense must be implanted in the dog from puppyhood. Here a Golden Retriever sits obediently at heel, waiting for the traffic to clear.

places to empty its bladder and bowels.

This type of training does not change the basic character of the puppy, for the dog is a pack animal and through training procedures it comes to regard its master as the pack leader. Such a unique relationship, which is built up only through regular and careful training sessions, helps to establish the puppy as an acceptable member within the family unit.

Learning its name

One of the first words the puppy must learn is its name. Choose a suitable name for your puppy as soon as you acquire it and stick to this name for the rest of its life. Try not to use 'Pup' at first, tempting though it is, and do not change names after a week or two or your pet will become thoroughly confused. A short one-syllable name is best or a simple flowing two-syllable one. The name should not sound similar to any of the command words that will be used in training. These words include 'No', 'Come', 'Sit', 'Wait', 'Stay', 'Down', 'Leave', and 'Heel'.

From the start, call your puppy by name in a gentle, coaxing and pleased tone of voice. Attract its attention with hand or arm movements that suggest a game is possible, like clapping your hands, slapping your leg, and so on. If the puppy ignores you wait until it has finished whatever it is doing, then try

again when it is more likely to respond. Giving a command when there is little chance of success merely reinforces disobedience. Always wait until the critical moment when the puppy looks as though it will come to you. Call it and then, when it does respond, make a fuss of it. This is one of the most important lessons of your puppy's life.

If your pup is rather wilful or aloof and it fails to come, try turning and walking slowly away. This usually produces the desired response. As soon as the puppy obeys, praise it and finish the lesson. Repeat the lesson regularly, adding the word 'Come!' in a friendly but authoritative tone, until you are confident that your puppy will come whenever you ask. Never fail to reward with praise and never let the puppy become bored with lessons. Avoid calling your puppy by name when it is necessary to scold or punish, as this would only confuse it. The pup's name should always be associated with pleasant experiences so that the dog will answer to it at all times.

The meaning of 'No!'

Once a young puppy has completed its vaccination programme it should be encouraged to mix with lots of people outside the family circle. It should be accustomed to contact with other animals and be gradually introduced to all types of noises and strange situations. Teach it the meaning of the word 'No!', which must always be spoken in a firm, stern voice every time the puppy does something unacceptable. This command is an important one that must be taught correctly from the very beginning. Never use it unless you can be sure it will be obeyed, and reinforce the word with a raised, reproving index finger. If a puppy ignores this command, repeat it and physically stop the dog from doing the misdeed.

Encourage the very young puppy to pick up and carry small articles. It is the easiest time to encourage this behaviour and leads naturally to the lessons in retrieval in later weeks. At this age plenty of praise is essential for good performance and helps to compensate for the many times it is necessary to use the 'No!' command. Even the most happy-go-lucky puppy prefers a petting to the stern chastisement of 'No!'. Puppies vary considerably in temperament; some are delighted with just a

Small puppies will chew at anything to relieve their gums as their sharp little teeth erupt. Special teething toys and rawhide 'chews' are preferable to pieces of wood, which can splinter.

A puppy given an old shoe as a toy may steal and chew its owner's shoes too. It must be sharply corrected, and given a toy as a substitute.

short word of praise and a pat on the head, but others need to be greatly fussed to encourage good behaviour. Refrain from using titbits as rewards during training. Most dogs consider their trainers as pack-leaders, and as they really want to please, kind words are sufficient reward.

Some dog-training manuals advocate the use of a rolled-up newspaper as a correction aid. Although its use will not hurt the puppy and may in some cases help to reinforce the command word given, an extrovert dog may regard the waving newspaper as an invitation to play rather than a mild punishment. With a nervous or intro-vert puppy, the use of a newspaper for correction could engender resentment or aggressiveness.

Temperament

It is possible to train any type of dog, and a young mongrel may prove to be just as responsive to instruction as a pedigree pup. Some individuals and a few specific breeds tend to learn more readily than others, but it is a mistake to think that the more intelligent dog will necessarily respond most willingly to human commands. A highly intelli-gent dog may be inclined to resent each new exercise to which it is introduced, treating it with suspicion until its fears are allayed. Such dogs will perform an exercise only when they have been convinced that there is some point in doing it.

Some dogs have the aptitude to achieve high standards in obedience work, while shy or nervous dogs may be able to master only a few simple exer-cises. The dog's temperament is an extremely important factor. The best type of dog for training is one that has an equable nature and a bold, fearless outlook on life. Some dogs may have been badly reared, ill-treated as pup-pies, or may never have been properly

integrated into family life. For these reasons they will remain introverted animals – but they can still be trained with love and patience.

Play

The importance of play cannot be overemphasised. It is vital in preparing the young puppy both physically and mentally for adult life. When a puppy is taken from its canine family and made a part of your own, you will need to continue some of the games the young dog has come to enjoy. The commonest form of puppy play is the mock fight in which puppies in a litter engage in rough-and-tumble battles with each other. You can play such a game with your puppy. Taking care not to be too rough, push and roll it around on the floor, grasping the loose skin of the neck from time to time and giving it a little shake. The puppy will back off, then growl and pounce on your hand and arm and thoroughly enjoy the game. Never pull your hand sharply back, however, or the pup's sharp teeth could snag your skin. The puppy will snap, chew, and gnaw at your hand, but it will never close its jaws because the threats are all bluff. This form of play is designed to build up muscles and develop the reflexes. Another puppy game is 'tag', when young dogs take turns to chase one another. Here again you, as owner, can take the place of a litter mate and establish an excellent relationship with your dog.

It is imperative that your dog should both respect and really love you if you are to achieve good results from later training. The close relationship that develops from the early sharing of games gives an excellent start. When playing doggy games try to think and act like a dog yourself. Do not let the puppy become over-excited. The 'No!' command can be given to restrain its exuberance followed by praise and reward when the little dog relaxes.

Travelling by car

The sooner your puppy gets used to car travel, the better. From the very start, take the puppy with you whenever you have to make short journeys by car, such as to the grocery store or post office, for example. Cover the seats with newspapers and an old towel at first, just in case the dog is inclined to travel sickness. Always allow at least three hours to elapse after the last meal before setting out on a journey, and give the puppy a chance to exercise and empty itself before departure. From time to time put the puppy in the car while it is parked outside your home, making sure that the windows are wound down sufficiently to let fresh air in, but not so low that the puppy can escape. If the puppy is nervous at first, try feeding it in the car, and see that it has its own blanket and a favourite toy to play with.

Most dogs love riding in cars and get very excited when they think a trip is imminent. Your dog must be trained to sit on its allocated seat or on the floor.

Above *Puppies love to play with one another, chasing and engaging in mock battles. Here one youngster assumes a dominant posture, while the other submits.*

Right *Dog-guards fitted behind the back seats of estate cars prevent dogs from jumping over the seats and distracting the driver's attention.*

It must never be allowed to ride along with its head hanging out of the window, as this can cause serious inflammation of the eyes. Your dog should not leap in and out of the car, and it will need to learn the 'Sit!' and 'Wait!' commands. The dog must be trained to sit quietly on the lead and wait patiently until told to get into the car. It is even more important to train your dog to keep sitting quietly inside the car when the door is opened, and to wait calmly until it is allowed to get out. It is very dangerous indeed if a boisterous dog leaps out in an uncontrolled way every time the car door opens. However, acceptable car behaviour can be instilled in even the most wilful and wayward of young dogs.

Car sickness in dogs is often best cured by familiarisation. This can be accomplished by making regular short trips so that the animal becomes accustomed to the vehicle's motion. If the problem persists, ask for travel tablets from your veterinary surgeon and withhold all food from your dog for several hours before setting off on a journey. (Advice on giving tablets, page 25.)

Be sure to take your dog's drinking bowl and a bottle of fresh water on long journeys. Plan to stop every hour or so to enable your pet to take a short walk and have a drink. If you own an estate car and habitually travel long distances with your dog, or if you plan to take it on holiday, you may wish to fit a dog-guard screen to the rear area, effectively converting it into a comfortable kennel and preventing the dog from clambering over the other seats. It is also possible to buy a special grid which fits in the top of an open side window. It allows good air flow when the car is parked yet prevents the dog escaping.

Training classes

The majority of dog owners are quite satisfied if their dog is well-behaved in the home, allows itself to be groomed, comes when it is called, and walks obediently on the lead. Others would like to enlarge on this repertoire but are not sure how to begin. Some people have problem dogs which refuse to come when called or are difficult to handle in other ways. For these owners, and those who would like to learn more about dogs, there are dog-training classes and clubs in most towns. Such classes generally enrol dogs from six months of age onwards. If possible, try to arrange to go along as an observer only, taking your puppy too if it is allowed, so that you can get an insight into the sort of procedures to expect. Normal training classes teach you how to train your own dog and give the animal the chance to socialise in a controlled way with others of its species. Preliminary classes cover all the basic commands; the more advanced classes are for those who wish to progress to the higher levels of obedience work to competition standard.

Although you will learn valuable lessons at each class, do not expect miracles to happen. It is up to you to use the knowledge intelligently, perhaps in a modified way if you feel that would be more appropriate in your case. The secret of success in training, however, is to reinforce the lessons with daily practice. Many 'failures' in class result from the fact that the owner of the wayward dog has not bothered to carry on with 'homework' between classes.

Serious training

Proper training should begin when your puppy is between six and eight months old. Start by fitting it with a good quality check collar of the correct size, and put this on just before you start the daily lesson. Whether the lesson is at home or at training class, allow your dog a good romp beforehand to get rid of its excess bounce. Three or four hours should be allowed to elapse after the dog's last meal before the lesson is given. Never start a training session if you are short of time or are feeling tired or tense. Always embark upon a lesson with a positive, optimistic attitude. Lessons need only be as long as 20 minutes; and the odd lesson can be worked in with other things, such as a play period, when it need only last about five minutes.

Your puppy will be used to walking on a collar and lead, possibly in an untrained and boisterous way, and should already know its name. It will have come to love and trust you, treating you as the leader of its family pack and so proper training can begin. All early training should be carried out on the lead, for it is pointless to try to teach the puppy to obey a command unless you can enforce it.

Right *At an outdoor training class students learn correct methods of canine control. Here the dogs have been told to assume the 'Down' position, then to 'Stay' as the handlers move away.*

Fitting a check chain

When it is correctly fitted, as here, the check chain will act as an ideal device for checking your dog.

When it is incorrectly fitted, as here, the check chain cannot release correctly and may tend to choke the dog.

'Come!'

This simple exercise to teach your puppy to come when called can be used at the start of each lesson. Fit the training check collar and a long training lead and have your dog at your left-hand side. Walk smartly forward and allow the dog to walk or trot ahead of you. Call its name and say 'Come!' invitingly, at the same time walking backwards and pulling the slack lead towards you. The first two or three times you do this, you may need to give the lead a smart jerk to attract the dog's attention and to encourage it to follow you; but very soon the dog will come to enjoy this almost as a game, and will bound towards you with pleasure. Give it lots of praise.

The release word

Before you continue with true training, you need to decide on a 'release' word or phrase which you can use every time you wish to release your dog from the position in which you have left it. Some trainers say 'Okay!', some prefer 'Paid For!' or 'Free Now!'; but whatever you choose, make sure that it cannot be confused with any of the command words that you intend to use during training. The release word may be accompanied by a physical release, and the well-trained adult dog can be taught to respond to either the word, the gesture, or a combination of the two. The release word is used when you feel that the dog has performed well during training and you have praised or rewarded it. When it is praised or rewarded the dog must not relax its position; but the release word indicates that it may now romp or play.

It is now time to teach the basic 'Sit!', 'Stay!', 'Down!', and 'Wait!' commands as well as correct walking at heel. Keep the lessons short and well structured. Start each new lesson by reinforcing the ones mastered the previous day. Make all the lessons enjoyable; never continue with an exercise when your dog is tired, bored, or distracted by circumstances beyond your control. Put a check collar on your dog before you begin and try to use the same training lead for every lesson. Your dog should enjoy learning and show signs of excitement when the training equipment is produced.

Right *Praise is an essential part of the training sequence and should be given as shown, rather than by rewarding the dog with titbits.*

Main picture *One of the most important lessons of all for the young dog is to learn to come to its owner every time it is called. This exercise is taught first by having the dog on a long training lead, and encouraging it to come forward eagerly whenever it is asked to do so.*

'Heel!' and 'Sit!'

In teaching your dog to walk at heel you want it to stride eagerly along on your left-hand side with its right shoulder adjacent to your left knee. Fit the check collar correctly so that it can be tightened or slackened at will. Attach it to the training lead. Hold the spare length of lead in your right hand and level with your waist. It should have a slight loop in it so that no tension is exerted on the check collar. To start the exercise, give the command 'Heel!' in a firm and business-like manner, jerk the lead very slightly and move off with the left foot. Your stride should be short and bouncy and the pace fairly brisk. Keep your left hand free of the lead and use it to encourage the dog to keep close by tapping your left thigh or clicking your fingers. You may find it helpful to carry a small article in your left hand to keep your dog interested – one of its favourite squeaky toys, perhaps, or a biscuit. Avoid grabbing at

your dog as this could make it hand-shy, which is difficult to cure.

Start by walking in straight lines. If your dog is inclined to pull to the left, walk alongside a fence or wall. Repeat the command 'Heel!' from time to time, using a pleasant tone and chat to your dog while it walks along. Keep the dog constantly alert and do not let its attention wander from the lesson. If it drags behind, bring the action of the check collar into use. Give the lead a short sharp jerk to bring the dog forward, repeat 'Heel!' and keep on walking. You may need to repeat this once or twice. When the dog comes forward to the correct position, give it verbal praise.

Some dogs persistently pull forward on the lead during heel-work training but it is a great mistake to try to counteract this by pulling on the lead. If you do this, the walk will become a trial of strength with you and the dog pulling against each other. When the dog is walking correctly, the lead will

be slightly slack; as soon as it pulls forward, give a reminder on the check collar by taking the slack of the lead in the left hand and jerking it sharply backwards. Your dog will soon learn that it is most comfortable to trot along at your side, and that pulling forward or hanging back results in an unpleasant jerk on its neck.

Every time you decide to stop, put your dog into a sitting position on your left side, facing forward, and with its right shoulder still near your left knee. To encourage it to sit from the walk, give the 'Sit!' command, raise your right hand to keep the dog's head high and lean over and use your left hand to push down on the dog's rump. The 'Sit!' command should be given in a

There are few things more annoying than a dog that pulls on its lead, and most dogs soon learn to walk correctly at heel. Here the young German Shepherd follows its handler's changes of direction and maintains the correct position.

firm voice and slightly drawn out, emphasising the 't'. Insist on instant reaction from your dog in this exercise. Do not accept sloppy results with the dog swivelling around to sit sideways, half sitting, going right down or rolling over. Repeat the 'Heel!' and walk for a few paces, then repeat the 'Sit!'. Try to avoid giving the commands at the same points in the garden as it is important to prevent your dog from connecting landmarks with commands.

When the dog sits correctly and you have praised it, wait a moment, and then give your release word in a pleased voice along with your chosen release gesture, best given with a gentle tap of the foot to a small dog or a nudge with the knee. Using hand gestures for release is not a good idea, as you use your hands for praise and reward and the dog could misunderstand your wishes. Most dogs enjoy being released and leap around excitedly like small boys let out of school.

When your dog walks well to heel on straight lines, start teaching it right-hand and left-hand circles. Begin by walking in a fairly large circle to the right. Encourage the dog to keep close to your left knee by giving slight jerks with the lead in your right hand, slapping your thigh in encouragement with your left, and continually repeating the 'Heel!' command. Continue to reinforce the 'Sit' exercise while working on the circle, give lots of praise when the work goes well, but stop and start again if it seems to be going badly. Try not to scold poor results at first. It is better to ignore bad work and immediately praise the dog when it gets it right. Never let the lesson go on until the dog becomes bored. If things have gone badly, go back to an earlier exercise such as walk to heel on a straight line, put the dog in the sit position, give it praise, and release it for the day.

Walking in a left-hand circle is more difficult, and it is all too easy to fall over your dog until it understands just what is required. It helps if there is some sort of guiding line around which you can steer the dog; your parked car would do, or some garden chairs arranged in a circle. Start with the dog sitting at your side in the usual manner. Give the 'Heel!' command and move off with your left foot. Raise the lead slightly with your left hand to guide the dog over to the left if necessary; take longer strides than normal and use your left leg to ease the dog's head and neck into the left-handed circle you require. As soon as you achieve a satisfactory result, praise the dog and end the lesson. Repeat it at the start of the next

day's session. Be sure to add lots of sit exercises on these circles, and remember to give the commands at different places each time.

At about this stage in the training, your dog may be getting lax about its sitting position and slow in assuming it. It is important to expect accurate and instant responses at all times, and if you praise the dog for a movement that it has not performed well you will have reinforced the error. Once made and allowed to pass, mistakes are hard to erase; if they are also rewarded with a pat, they may never be erased. If your dog does get lazy about the 'Sit!' command, some stern effort is required to put it right. Walk briskly forward with the dog at heel, give it the order to 'Sit!', jerk up the head slightly with the check collar and press down the dog's rump; ensure that the dog is pressed

The 'Sit' lessons begins with the dog sitting down, its right shoulder close against the handler's left leg. Hold the dog's head in position with the lead, and simultaneously press down the hindquarters, with the command 'Sit!'.

well up against your left leg. Walk on and repeat this several times, giving praise when it is well performed. The first time it is done perfectly, praise the dog and release it.

Practise heel-work daily, and prevent boredom by varying your pace, walking in zig-zags, serpentines and figures-of-eight as well as in straight lines, squares with sharp corners, and alternate circles. Although it might seem difficult at first, with correctly given praise words and the proper use of the check collar, both you and your dog will become extremely proficient.

'Sit and Stay'

When your dog sits well on a verbal command and no longer needs the additional aids of lead and hands, proceed to the 'Sit and Stay' exercise. Tell the dog to 'Sit!' in the normal way, then let the slack of the lead loop down to the ground and change the end of the lead from your right to your left hand. Show the dog the palm of your right hand by holding it near its face and give a firm and slightly drawn-out command, 'Stay!'. Repeat the word, hold the hand towards the dog and take a long slow step to your right. Extend the left arm so that the lead does not pull the dog towards you. The dog should remain sitting and watching you. Repeat the word 'Stay!' and reverse your step until you are next to your dog once more. If the dog does not move, praise it and repeat the exercise once or twice more, but keep this first lesson quite short. If the dog does move either to lie down or to follow you to the right, put it back in position and try again. Punish movement with a stern 'No!' before re-positioning the dog with the 'Sit!' command. Repeat this exercise daily; when the dog seems really steady, develop the movement.

This is done in stages. The first progression is carried out by looping the end of the long training lead onto the thumb of your left hand. Sit the dog in the usual position, give the 'Stay!' command and take the long step to your right. Fully extend your left arm so that your hand is virtually over the dog's head. Using your left thumb as a pivot point, slowly walk anti-clockwise right around your dog until you are back in the normal training position once more. The dog must not move. If it does, start again from the beginning and revert to the original Sit and Stay exercise if necessary until you achieve a positive result, then praise profusely and release the dog. Work the Sit and Stay exercise in with daily heel-work and random sits so that the dog has variety in its exercises.

When you are confident it will stay in the Sit position while you circle round, try the Stay without the lead. Practise first of all by putting the end of the lead on the ground while you ask for the 'Stay!' and take your long step to the right. If this is successful, walk in a circle around your dog and return to the training position. If your work is progressing in a satisfactory manner the dog will remain motionless; if you are rushing things or have a slow or wilful dog, go back to a previous stage and work up to the 'Stay!' once more.

The next stage is to remove the lead while the dog is at Sit and Stay and to walk away. Always take the side step first before moving forward so your dog does not think it should go forward at heel. It should, by now, connect your sideways step with remaining motionless, and your left-foot-forward step with going to heel.

Walk only a few paces away from your dog at first and keep repeating the 'Stay!' command in a calm and steady-ing manner. Always return to the training position before praising the dog, then either continue with a new exercise or give the release. Vary your procedure so that the release is never anticipated and the dog waits for your next instruction at all times. When you and your pet have mastered this exercise, you will have reached an important stage in training, and your dog will realise that 'Stay!' always means that you are going to return to its side.

Above *Begin 'Sit and Stay' exercises by telling the dog to sit; reinforce command with palm of right hand. Then (left) take a long, slow step away from dog. Make sure the lead remains slack (right) and repeat command and palm gesture before stepping back to the dog's side again.*

Right *Next stage in exercise: loop the end of the training lead over the left thumb, take one step away from the dog, then walk slowly around it.*

Below *The third stage repeats the operation of walking around the dog, but this time at the full extent of the training lead. Finally, the exercise is done without the lead.*

'Wait!' and 'Come!'

When you want the dog to remain in its position and then to come to you when you call, you must teach a different word to avoid complete confusion in the animal's mind. 'Wait!' is a very important command, and must be thoroughly and correctly taught from the outset. The easiest way to start this exercise is to sit the dog in the normal way, praise it a little, then move quietly round in front of it. Place your right hand in front of the dog's nose, showing the palm, and say 'Wait!' in a low and drawn-out way. Holding the end of the slackened training lead in your left hand, take small steps backwards away from your dog, repeating the command, until you get to the end of the lead. If the dog remains motionless, call its name and say 'Come!' in a pleased and welcoming way. Give a little pull on the lead if it seems reluctant to obey.

When the dog reaches you, praise it and try to get it to sit facing you.

If all goes well, the 'Wait!' command can be given again while you move back once more to reinforce the lesson. If the dog moves forward as you start to reverse, you must begin again, taking one small step at a time. If you think the Sit position is going to be broken, you can pre-empt your dog by giving the 'Come!' command just before it rises from its haunches. This exercise must be taken very slowly and built-in to the previous programme without letting your dog get bored. Only when it is completely mastered should you go on to the next stage.

Replace the training lead with a long thin cord so that you can extend your distance from your dog while remaining in control should it decide to move away from its sitting position. Always make your 'Come!' command as welcoming as possible, and fuss your dog in its favourite way whenever it responds correctly. A titbit encourages some dogs, especially those of wilful or scatter-brained breeds which are easily distracted. Keep a favourite biscuit or liver treat in the palm of your hand and make sure your dog knows that it is there. In the 'Come!' exercise, recall your dog and add an arm gesture by either holding your hand up to your chest or extending your arms. If the hand with the titbit is held up to your chest, the dog is likely to race towards you and sit immediately, looking up at your face expectantly, hoping for the titbit. Do not give a titbit every time; vary the reward so that your dog does not require constant food bribes in order to perform correctly.

When you are certain that the dog will come to you from the Wait position when you recall it, remove the cord. If you have some failures and your dog runs off or will not come right up to you, revert to more controlled methods for a while.

At this stage, your young dog should be giving you a great deal of satisfaction, walking to heel at all paces, sitting when told and staying on command until your return. The Wait response can be developed further to keep the dog from running or jumping forward until it is called. This is particularly useful, on country walks when you have to cross streams or ditches or open difficult gates, and it is a means of preventing your dog from exuberantly leaping into and out of your car. It is useful, too, on the return home when the dog has muddy feet and you want it to remain outside the house while you go in first to fetch a towel.

'Down and Stay'

Once your dog reaches this point in training, you are ready to teach the 'Down!' command. If you have the sort of dog that was apt to collapse in a heap every time you wanted it to sit, you may find that it is slightly bewildered by the fact that you now want it to take up that previously unacceptable position. Teach your dog to lie down on command by pulling the lead forward, giving the command 'Down!' in a low voice and, if necessary, getting down on the ground with the dog. With a large dog you may gently pull its forelegs forward and press down on its shoulder blades until it is in the desired position. Praise the dog when it is down correctly. If it persists in getting up, persevere until you are successful. Spend several days on this exercise. Only when your dog goes into the down position promptly and without any fuss should you progress to the 'Down and Stay' exercise.

This is taught in exactly the same way as the Sit and Stay. Use a loosely looped lead and step away to the dog's right then walk slowly around in a circle. Praise the dog only when it remains in the down position; if it deviates from this, start from the beginning again. End the lesson as soon as you achieve the desired result. Never recall your dog from the Down position. It should be fixed in its mind as a stationary posture and one you will return to presently and give the release. Down and Stay are static positions; 'Wait!', however, means that another command is to come.

In teaching 'Down', the lead is pulled forward and the dog's shoulders are firmly pushed down until it assumes the correct position in a relaxed attitude.

If your dog has successfully performed all these exercises it will have reached an acceptable level for a family dog. Try and perfect these simple exercises until your dog happily responds both on and off the lead. The Down exercise should be practised frequently and at length, until your dog immediately drops down at your command, no matter what it is doing. This training can save a dog's life, for it will enable the animal to be controlled from a distance, perhaps when a hazardous situation unexpectedly arises.

'Leave!'

The command 'Leave!' can also be a life-saver. The object of the exercise is to teach your dog to leave an object alone until you release it with another simple command.

A good way of teaching the lesson is to show the dog a favourite treat, like a tasty biscuit, but make the animal leave it alone until it is told it may have it. Put the dog on its check collar and lead, and hold it in check with your left hand. Start at the Sit position, where

the dog is more easily controlled than if it is standing. Show the dog the biscuit and say 'Leave!' in a very commanding voice. Put the treat on the ground just out of the animal's reach. The dog will naturally go to take the biscuit but you must pull him back with a short jerk, repeating the 'Leave!' command. When you wish the dog to take the biscuit use a different release word. If 'Okay!' is your normal release, use 'Paid For!' or 'Fetch it!'. Dogs quickly learn this exercise and before long you will be able to add refinements such as rolling

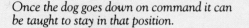

Once the dog goes down on command it can be taught to stay in that position.

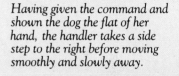

Having given the command and shown the dog the flat of her hand, the handler takes a side step to the right before moving smoothly and slowly away.

The stay command is constantly repeated and reinforced by the hand signal until the handler has reached the limit of the training lead's length.

Left *As the dog gains confidence and develops, more refined exercises may be added to its training programme, and the first step in retrieval may be taught. Here the handler asks the dog to wait (her left foot is placed on top of the training rope) while she prepares to throw the dumb-bell with her left hand.*

The lead is then taken in the right hand and the dog is sent to retrieve.

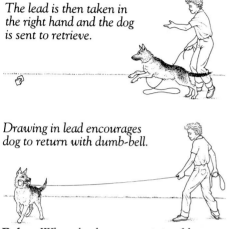

Drawing in lead encourages dog to return with dumb-bell.

Below *When the dog returns it is told to sit, the dumb-bell is gently removed, and the dog is praised.*

the biscuit past your dog, or even throwing it, and it will not be pounced upon and eaten until you indicate that it is allowed to do so.

The exercise can be expanded to include all sorts of things like thrown and rolled balls, for example. Dogs can be prevented from being destructive by learning this command. 'Leave!' can be shouted from the bedroom window when you notice your pet digging up your rose bush or about to chase the neighbour's cat. It can prevent the inquisitive dog from being stung by bees or wasps and from stealing cake from the tea-table. As usual, however, it is important that your dog obeys the command instantly and without question, knowing that it will eventually receive a reward.

The retrieve

Many dogs have a natural instinct to retrieve objects. It presumably dates back to their ancestors' wild state when food was carried to the den. Some gundogs are bred for their propensity to retrieve, and such breeds can be trained very easily. A young puppy should be encouraged to carry its toys around in its mouth; if however, it has been scolded for doing so, the animal will be more difficult to teach in this exercise.

Train the retrieve by having your dog on a long line or cord and sitting at your left-hand side. Throw a suitable article, either a proper training dumb-bell or a piece of wood of similar size, and give the 'Fetch!' command in an encouraging manner. The dog should run and pick up the article. Once this has occurred, gently pull the line and give the 'Come!' command. When the dog responds, ask it to sit in front of you and praise it for holding the article well. Take the dumb-bell or wood in both hands, give a command such as 'Drop it!', and gently remove the article from the dog's jaws. Take care not to hurt your pet's mouth in removing the object, and praise it profusely for a job well done. It is a short progression to working off the lead, and then to training the dog to fetch any article that is pointed to. If a young dog excitedly races about with the object retrieved, you must go back to an earlier stage of the exercise.

Further training

When your dog has achieved a good standard of basic training you will have some idea of its potential. If you are interested in learning more refined and advanced training techniques for your dog you should contact your veterinary surgeon or local council offices to find out about dog-training and obedience classes in your area. You will have learnt a lot about your dog during the basic training exercises and you will have added many important lessons of your own. Your pet will now know, often by your voice and general attitude, if you are pleased or displeased, and will attempt to behave in a way that elicits praise, not punishment.

Tricks

If your dog responds readily to its lessons you might like to teach it a few party tricks. Never, however, encourage your pet to perform in a way that makes it appear undignified or foolish. The teaching of tricks should be carried out only after your dog has completely mastered its basic training and can be relied on to be obedient and well-behaved in all situations.

Tricks are taught by encouraging the desired behaviour in small stages and giving rewards when properly performed. Unlike basic training, which rewards with verbal praise and a pat, tricks are normally rewarded with a favourite titbit.

The most popular trick of all is to make the dog sit up. It is only suitable for small to medium sized dogs of the right conformation. Dogs with very long backs or long legs find it virtually impossible to balance while sitting up on their haunches, and it is unkind to try to teach them to do so. Terriers love to beg and are very easy to teach. Wait until your puppy is at least six months old, then start by holding a tempting titbit just out of reach over its head. Say 'Sit up!' in a pleasant but firm manner, and lift the pup's front end with your other hand. Find the point of balance and repeat the command, simultaneously giving the reward. It does not take a perceptive puppy long to grasp this trick, and it is soon sitting up appealingly at every opportunity. Do not reward this behaviour while you are having meals or else your dog will become such a meal-time pest that it will have to be banished from the room. Reward sitting up only when you have actually given the verbal command and not when the dog does it voluntarily.

As your dog grows up, you may notice little habits which can be developed naturally into its own particular tricks. Some dogs are able to throw objects; some, notably the retrieving breeds, enjoy carrying articles in their mouths; others learn to lift a rug and hide an article underneath. These actions are merely variations of normal canine behaviour and can be expanded by encouragement and reward, with suitable and recognisable command words or signals to indicate when they should be carried out.

It is simple to teach your dog to 'Die for the Queen!', encouraging it to stretch out on its side and stay motionless; or to 'Roll Over!' and expose its tummy for a friendly rub. Carrying a shopping basket or a folded newspaper are natural progressions from the retrieve of basic training, as is the 'Go Seek!' trick when the dog has to find a hidden article.

For all these tricks, the dog is first shown what to do and is praised for each new stage of the trick that it masters. All tricks are taught in gradual stages. Every time you experience a setback, it merely means that your dog does not understand what you want, so you must regress one stage. Each lesson should finish with a success, no matter how small it may be.

Left *This little terrier has been taught to sit up and beg its owner to give it the dish of food. Although small dogs can assume this position quite easily, it may be an unsafe one for large breeds.*

Right *Dogs often enjoy carrying articles in their mouths, and this trait can often be exploited by the keen owner. This intelligent dog, for example, has been taught to fetch his deep plastic bowl on command before each of its meal-times.*

How to Cure
Bad Habits

Pulling on lead

Dogs that habitually pull when on the lead can often be cured of this habit by use of a check chain. The dog must be made to walk to heel; then, whenever it pulls forwards or backwards, the chain is given a short, sharp jerk, and then released with the command 'Heel!' Many large dogs get very excited when they know they will shortly be taken for a walk. A quick run around the garden off the lead helps to take the edge off this over-excitement.

Destructive dogs

The puppy naturally chews things to help in the cutting of its second teeth, and because of this, it may well cause damage in the home. A young dog should never be left alone where it can spoil valuable property or furnishings. It should be confined within a playpen while you are out of the house and given its own toys and rawhide chews for company. Some adult dogs resent being left alone and become distressed, scratching at doors and carpet. Unless checked, this behaviour may develop into determined tearing and chewing. It is pointless to punish such misdeeds as soon as you arrive home, because the dog will be so pleased to see you that the punishment will seem to the dog to be linked with the exuberance of its greeting. If you expect to leave your dog alone for long periods, you should prevent the onset of destructive behaviour by early training.

If the problem has become ingrained you have several alternative solutions. The first and most obvious is never to leave your dog alone. You may have the sort of job which enables you to take your pet to work. Other dogs give up destructive behaviour if they are allowed the complete run of the house, but it may be impracticable to try this out for the first few days, especially if you have valuable belongings. The third alternative is to buy a second dog. When the two animals become friends you will probably find that all destructive behaviour ceases completely.

Positive action is needed to retrain a destructive dog. Start by leaving the room and closing the door. Return a minute later and check for damage; if there is none, praise the dog. If some damage has been caused, make a point of examining it but totally ignore your dog. Do not punish the dog as that will

Pages 56–7 This Old-English Sheepdog has forgotten all its early training and bursts out of the front door in its eagerness to go for its walk.

not help matters. Sooner or later – and you may need a lot of patience – the dog will be left for a short period without doing any damage. This is the breakthrough point. Take care to extend the periods of isolation very, very gradually until the dog is retrained and may confidently be left alone.

Wandering dogs

If your dog persistently jumps over the garden fence and runs away for the day, you have every right to be concerned. No dog should be allowed to roam free, for no matter how well-behaved it is at home, you have no means of knowing what it would do in an unusual situation. It could do a lot of wilful damage or cause a serious road accident.

Dogs naturally give chase to anything that runs away from them and a dog that likes to chase sheep may have to be destroyed. Sheep have an excitable effect on most dogs. They look vulnerable and run away in an inviting sort of way, often turning to look back at the dog. A great deal of harm can be done to such valuable livestock when they are chased around: pregnant ewes drop premature lambs, for example, and other sheep become so distressed that they may die of heart failure. Dogs sometimes gang up and methodically hunt down a sheep before savaging it to death – an example of ancient instincts coming to the fore despite centuries of domestication. It is virtually impossible to teach an ordinary family dog not to chase farm animals so you must therefore ensure that your dog always remains under your control. Keep it on a lead during country walks, and if it likes to lope around and explore, use a long cord or line in place of the normal lead. Heighten the fence at home if your dog is able to jump it, or keep your pet on an extendable running line when it is left alone in the garden. Such lines fit easily onto an outside wall. The end is clipped to the dog's collar and the line pulls out of the holder as the dog runs around. Any slack is drawn back in so that there is no chance of the animal becoming entangled.

Jumping up

An exuberant dog will often run up to visitors and friends and jump up against them, trying to get its mouth as close as possible to the visitor's face. While this is natural behaviour for the dog, it is usually unacceptable to people, particularly if the dog has been romping in the garden and has muddy paws. Jumping up is easily corrected in any dog, but the sooner it is done the better. Have the dog on a check collar and a

long training lead or length of line and set up the situation beforehand with an assistant. The assistant should walk naturally in through the front gate, for example, or through a door. The dog will run forward as usual in greeting. Just as the dog starts to jump up, jerk the lead hard and command a very stern 'No!' Give the 'Sit!' command, and if it is obeyed the assistant can make a fuss of the dog. This may have to be repeated a few times, but in most cases the dog will quickly learn acceptable manners.

If your dog runs up to you and jumps up, the check collar will be of little use. The easiest way to stop this behaviour is to bring your knee up into the dog's chest at the moment it jumps forward. While it is still bewildered by this unkindness, give the 'Sit!' command, then praise the dog. Here again the younger dog should learn very quickly. The lesson, once learned, should never be relaxed, and neither should anyone be allowed to encourage your dog to go onto its hind legs.

Right *A dog that jumps up at visitors, although it may simply be showing affection, can be frightening and may cause injury and damage to clothing. The habit can be cured as shown below.*

You need a friend to help with this training. As the friend comes through the gate, the dog is restrained from jumping up by firm use of the lead.

Restraint of the dog is accompanied by a firm 'No!', then the 'Sit!' command. When the dog responds instantly to the check, the 'visitor' should praise it.

Chasing vehicles

Chasing cars and bicycles is a bad habit which should be stopped promptly before a serious accident occurs. Dogs should never be allowed to roam the streets freely, and it is also dangerous if a dog on its lead tries to leap at passing vehicles. To break this aggressive habit, attach a training collar and lead and take the dog to a stretch of road where the traffic is fairly heavy, there are few pedestrians and the pavement is reasonably wide. Make your dog sit correctly on your left side and wait quietly for the first car to pass. As the dog starts to leap forward or bark, jerk it back on the check collar and give a severe 'No!' command. When this has had some effect, try walking with the dog at heel with traffic coming from behind. Correct impulsive forward moves by the dog until success is achieved. Finish the lesson on a positive note and take the dog home. Repeated and regular lessons are required until your dog is calm with all traffic. It is useful to have a friend ride past you on a bicycle each day while you train the dog to accept this experience in a similar way.

Chasing cats

Curing a dog of cat-chasing can be quite difficult. The best way undoubtedly is to have a dog-proof cat – a really tough and fearless animal which, instead of running away from the dog, fluffs up and gives it a good scratch across the sensitive end of its nose. If your dog chases your own cat you will need to work hard at trying to make them friends. Have your dog on the check collar and lead; every time the cat makes off and the dog leaps up in pursuit, jerk the lead and give a stern 'No!' command. Never encourage your dog to chase anything except a ball or toy that you have thrown, and scold it whenever it shows signs of running after birds in the garden.

Digging holes

All dogs love to dig. This innate behaviour dates back to the days when dogs buried the uneaten portion of their kill to hide it from other predators. Nowadays, bitches dig burrows in which to whelp, and overheated dogs dig earthy pits in which to cool off from the sun. As digging is a natural part of canine behaviour, it is very difficult to stop when it is done in an unacceptable place, like the middle of the lawn or around the prize roses. Try to distract the digging dog and give it some other exhausting exercise for a while. Give a firm 'No!' command every time it looks like starting an excavation. If these ruses are not effective, you will have to confine your dog to unimportant areas of the garden or buy a running chain or portable run.

Stealing food

It is perhaps asking rather a lot of the dog to expect it to sit patiently alone in a room where lots of tempting food is visible, and not to steal any. It is a different matter, however, when your dog habitually takes titbits from your kitchen work-surface or dining table when your attention is elsewhere for a moment or two. Teach your dog the 'Leave!' command and get it used to staying away from items of food when you have told it to do so. This behaviour can be reinforced by aversion therapy. Fill a soft chocolate or similar delicacy with a teaspoon of mustard and put it on the table. Give the 'Leave!' command then go out of the room for a moment. If the dog has left the decoy well alone, praise it profusely upon your return. If it has eaten the bait it will have had punishment enough. Some dogs swallow titbits so fast that they might not taste the mustard, in which case you should offer larger baits that need to be chewed. Repeat this procedure until your dog is convinced that all stolen food tastes awful. The mustard should deter your dog from stealing, but is not harmful when swallowed.

Some dogs cannot resist stealing sweets or cakes if left alone with them (right). To cure habitual stealing, a chocolate or cake may be filled with an unpleasant-tasting (but harmless) substance such as mustard, and then left as bait.

Barking

A dog that barks incessantly for no apparent reason is a nuisance and such behaviour must be stopped at once. Young puppies are unable to bark at all, and when they first learn to do so they often look surprised at the noise they manage to produce. Although it can be tempting to encourage the puppy to bark it is a mistake to do so and is difficult to correct later on. A dog will learn to bark aggressively when it feels that either itself or its property is being threatened. If the dog learns this naturally, barking will likely be kept to the minimum and you will know that a bark from your dog really does mean that a stranger is around and not that the animal is merely feeling a bit bored and wants some action. While you must accept the fact that your dog will bark when visitors arrive at your door, the animal must be trained to stop barking when you have admitted them to the house. The best way to do this is to slip the check collar and lead onto your dog while it is barking and the doorbell is ringing. Praise the dog, take it to the door and tell it to 'Sit!'. Open the door and invite your guests in while restraining the dog in the Sit position. Punish further barks with a stern 'No!', then allow your dog to meet and greet the visitors.

While it is acceptable for a dog to bark at the approach of strangers (left), incessant barking can be stopped by use of a check chain and the 'No!' command (above).

When the visitor enters, the dog is held back and ordered to sit. If it continues to bark, the check is reinforced and the 'No!' command repeated as necessary.

A dog that persistently barks when left alone in a room can be difficult to retrain. You must shut it in the room then creep away. Immediately it starts to bark, scold it with a series of severe 'No!' commands. This can be reinforced by clapping your hands as you give the commands. If it still has no effect you may have to punish the dog physically by shaking the scruff of its neck or even giving the animal a short sharp slap. The dog must understand that the reason for the punishment is its barking: any punishment must be given within 30 seconds of the offence if the animal is to link the two events.

Resentment of handling

Your dog may show resentment or even aggression when you attempt to touch a particular part of its body. If it has a coat that demands a lot of grooming and it has suffered at your hands through tugging at knots and tangles, this is quite understandable. It is up to you to undo the harm by gentle and careful retraining. It is extremely important for an owner to be able to handle his dog under any circumstances and at any time. At the scene of an accident, for example, ease of handling

Early handling from puppyhood ensures that dogs enjoy being fondled and allow examination of any parts of their heads and bodies. This 'Westie' (West Highland Light Terrier) obviously loves his young owner's attentions.

could mean the difference between life and death for your pet. If a puppy shows any resentment when a certain area is touched you will need to begin a familiarisation programme. Stroke or groom the sensitive part, talk soothingly to the puppy and praise it the moment it ceases to resist. Older dogs take a little longer to retrain, but with plenty of patience success can be achieved.

If a dog tends to snap during this type of training you may have to use a muzzle at first. Properly-made leather muzzles are available in all sizes and the one you choose should fit snugly. If it is too large the muzzle may slip off at the crucial moment; if it is too small it will hurt the dog and cause more resentment. If a muzzle is used, put it on the dog from time to time during normal playtime and exercise. Never let the dog connect the fitting of the muzzle with an unpleasant aspect of training.

Dog fights

Play fighting is first seen in young puppies of four to five weeks of age and it is these competitive trials of strength that lead to the formation of a social hierarchy. Most adult dogs avoid actual fights: males establish their territorial rights by urine-marking whenever possible and simply threaten other dogs by assuming various body postures like walking stiff-legged, holding the tail rigid, and perhaps giving a few warning growls.

When a serious fight breaks out between two dogs, most owners dive into the midst of the battle and try to separate their pets. This is foolish in the extreme and usually results in injuries to all those involved. Each owner should simultaneously pull his dog away by gripping it at the root of its tail. This must not be done however, if one dog has a firm grip with its teeth or else the other dog could suffer extensive damage. To make a dog release its hold, insert a forefinger into its rectum. The dog will react immediately to this and relax its grip. It should then be smartly pulled away from its adversary and prevented from returning to the attack. A bucket of cold water poured over two fighting dogs might force them apart, but they need to be quickly caught and controlled before they fall upon each other once more.

When two neighbouring dogs constantly threaten one another and are always spoiling for a fight, it is sometimes thought wise to let them sort out their battle for dominance once and for all. This was the practice on farms in the past when it was considered preferable to allowing feuds to continue. Certainly, once two dogs have settled the matter they need never fight again.

Coprophagia

The eating of faeces seems to us a most disgusting habit but some animals obtain valuable nourishment from it. For the wild dog, eating the droppings of large herbivores probably provides essential roughage and minerals as well as quantities of the B group of vitamins.

Members of a dog pack often eat part of each others faeces and also wash each others anal regions. This could help to ensure that all the pack members have the same types of micro-organisms living within their intestines, so preventing outbreaks of disease within the group. Most dogs grow out of coprophagia, especially when they learn that it upsets their owners. The veterinary surgeon can prescribe vitamin and mineral additives to an obsessive dog's diet, but the best cure is to keep the dog away from temptation by picking up and disposing of faeces as soon as they are voided.

Climbing on furniture

Many dogs will, if allowed, make for the most comfortable piece of furniture in your sitting room. A large dog can effectively monopolise the space on a good-sized sofa. If you do not wish your dog to sit on furniture, you will have to train him not to do so when he is still a young puppy. Even if you allow your dog to sit on a particular chair, it is as well to train him to vacate it instantly if he is ordered to do so. This, too, must be taught at an early age. Make sure that you use a command, such as 'Get off!', that will not be confused with 'Down!' or any other command used in basic training.

Most dogs enjoy resting on a luxurious bed, and they will often try to monopolise the most comfortable furniture unless they are corrected at an early age.

Don'ts for dog owners

Don't leave your dog alone for long periods during the day – he will get bored and may turn destructive!

Don't allow your dog to roam free: always make sure that your garden gates are closed and the garden as a whole is fully secure.

Don't give your dog an old slipper to play with – and then expect him not to chew your new shoes.

Don't leave your dog alone with children he does not know well.

Don't leave your dog in an unventilated car – and in sunny weather always park the car in shade.

Don't encourage your dog to chase cats or birds that visit the garden.

Don't vent your anger on your dog if it misbehaves: a reprimand is enough.

Don't punish misbehaviour unless you catch your dog at it – otherwise he will fail to connect the punishment with his misdeed.

Don't fail to enforce a command: it is useless saying 'No!' – and then allowing the dog to continue doing whatever it was you ordered him to stop doing.

Don't let your dog jump up or frighten visitors, however friendly his intentions may actually be.

Popular Dog Breeds

Pedigree dogs show more variation in size and shape, colour and coat texture, character and conformation than any other species of animal. This is due mainly to man's intervention in their breeding and development over the years. Basic canine characteristics were studied and selected for breeding, and so distinct types eventually evolved that were ideally suited to their allotted tasks as friends and servants of their masters.

Dogs today are divided into six main groups: Gundogs, Hounds, Terriers, Toys, Working Dogs, and Utility Dogs.

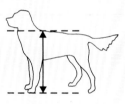

The dog sizes given in the tables on the following pages are those established for each breed by the Kennel Club of Great Britain. The figures for height denote the distance from ground to shoulder, as shown in the sketch above.

The words used in the tables to indicate the amount of exercise required by each breed can be defined as follows: Little: a daily romp with owner usually sufficient.

Moderate: at least half an hour's exercise daily, some of which should be off the lead.

Lots: a minimum of an hour's exercise every day, half of it running free.

Allow your dog to romp or run off the lead only where there is no danger from road vehicles. And remember that free running, however extensive, is no substitute for the daily period of play between a dog and its owner that is vital in developing the relationship between the two.

In the drawings on the following pages, all the dogs within a group are drawn to the same scale, but the scale varies from group to group.

The German Shepherd (often known as the Alsatian) is the most popular breed in Britain.

GUNDOGS

Breed and character	Typical size of male	Amount of exercise	Coat type	Amount of grooming	Guarding potential	Temperament with children	Possible problems
MÜNSTERLÄNDER, LARGE Loyal and trustworthy family pet; easy to train and a very good worker.	610 mm (24 in)	Lots	Long/dense	Regular	Poor	Very good	Ears inclined to get dirty unless cleaned regularly.
POINTER Good housedog and a fine gundog; affectionate and easily trained, gentle with other pets.	635–685 mm (25–27 in)	Lots	Short/fine	Little	Poor	Good	Very energetic.
RETRIEVER, GOLDEN Ideal family dog; loves retrieving. Often used as guide-dog for the blind.	560–610 mm (22–24 in)	Lots	Flat or wavy	Regular	Poor	Excellent	None.
RETRIEVER, LABRADOR Bright, alert, and friendly dog. Easily trained up to obedience standard; an excellent working dog.	560–570 mm (22–22½ in)	Lots	Short/dense	Little	Fair	Very good	Tends to overweight if not given plenty of exercise.
SETTER, ENGLISH Gentle, loving pet, easily trained. Can live indoors or outside.	635–685 mm (25–27 in)	Lots	Feathered	Lots	Poor	Very good	Coat tangles easily. Likes company.
SETTER, IRISH Beautiful, loving dog, good with other pets. Needs gentle early training.	685 mm (27 in)	Lots	Feathered	Lots	Poor	Very good	Coat tangles. Very energetic.
SPANIEL, COCKER Long-lived and easily trained pet, with a merry nature.	395 mm (15½ in)	Regular	Flat/silky	Lots	Fair	Very good	Ears tangle. Tends to overweight.
SPANIEL, SPRINGER Very alert and easily trained dog; affectionate and very lively.	510 mm (20 in)	Lots	Short/close	Regular	Fair	Very good	Ears may need attention. Tends to overweight.
VIZSLA Unusual russet-gold in colour. Excels as a gundog and makes a loving pet. Needs plenty of space fo free exercise.	570–635 mm (22½–25 in)	Lots	Short/dense	Little	Quite good	Quite good	Inclined to roam.
WEIMARANER Unusual pale colour. Responds well to careful training; excellent as a police dog and gundog.	610–685 mr (24–27 in)	Lots	Short/dense	Little	Quite good	Very good	Easily bored, can become destructive.

As their name implies, members of this group are eminently suited to the sporting life. They need a good deal of exercise and are easily trained as house pets. Generally of a kind and gentle disposition, most gundogs are good with children but not very effective as guards.

The first category within the Gundog group contains the Pointers and Setters, which were developed to locate and indicate the whereabouts of game. Spaniels form the second category. They were originally bred to flush out the game for sportsmen, by either forcing it into the air or driving it along the ground. The various breeds within this sub-group were developed to work in different conditions and types of terrain. Thirdly, there are the Retrievers, intelligent dogs with highly developed scenting powers, whose job was to fetch fallen game for their masters.

An English Pointer undergoes field training.

HOUNDS

This group of dogs is large and very diverse. It includes some that were developed to hunt their quarry by scent; others that were bred to chase and corner game, then to bay to call up the hunter; and specialised types for hunting large and ferocious animals. While some of the hounds have adapted well to family life, others remain aloof and would obviously prefer a working life. Many retain their hunting instincts and are not really suitable for keeping with other, smaller pets. Several breeds of hound make excellent guard dogs, some by virtue of their size and stature and others owing to their fearless character. Most hounds need plenty of exercise and space in which to run; all need careful discipline and training as puppies if they are to grow into suitable family pets.

The dapper, alert Beagle makes a cheerful companion.

Breed and character	Typical size of male	Amount of exercise	Coat type	Amount of grooming	Guarding potential	Temperament with children	Possible problems
AFGHAN HOUND Beautiful, glamorous dog, loyal to its own family. May have unreliable temper in adolescence.	685–735 mm (27–29 in)	Lots	Long/ Profuse	Lots	Good	Good unless teased	Can be aloof and independent.
BASENJI Clean dog lacking any 'doggie' odour, and it does not bark. Very gentle and affectionate.	430 mm (17 in)	Moderate	Short/ sleek	Little	Cannot bark	Very gentle	Aloof with strangers, and can be very mischievous.
BASSET HOUND Ideal family dog if kept in a well-fenced garden: independent but with a very lovable nature.	380 mm (15 in)	Lots	Short/fine	Little	Good	Very good	May roam, and tends to overweight. Can be disobedient.
BEAGLE Happy and affectionate pet, loyal and intelligent. Loves other pets.	Not under 330 mm (13 in) or over 405 mm (16 in)	Lots	Short/fine	Little	Quite good	Very good	May roam, and tends to overweight.
DACHSHUND, STANDARD Alert and active; may be rather strong-willed but makes a good pet.	10 kg (22 lb) 8·2 kg (18 lb) 11·3 kg (25 lb)	Moderate Moderate Moderate	Wire Long Smooth	Regular Lots Little	Good	Quite good	Inclined to overweight and spinal problems.
DACHSHUND, MINIATURE Self-willed but with careful early training it makes a good family pet.	Not over 5 kg (11 lb); ideal weight 4·5 kg (10 lb)	Enough to keep slim	Wire Long Smooth	Regular Lots Little	Good	Good	Inclined to overweight and spinal problems.
FINNISH SPITZ Brave, faithful, loving and sociable: an ideal family dog, and it has no 'doggie' odour.	445 mm (17½ in)	Moderate	Short/ stand-off	Little	Very good	Good	May be delicate as a young pup.
GREYHOUND Noble and gentle dog which repays kind treatment: affectionate to family, but needs firm control.	710–760 mm (28–30 in)	Lots/on lead	Short/ sleek	Little	Quite good	Gentle with kind ones	Retains its strong coursing tendencies.
IRISH WOLFHOUND Majestic hound, fierce when provoked. Can be wilful and needs careful training.	815 mm (32 in)	Moderate	Thick/ wiry	Regular	Very good	Excellent	May be over-protective. Needs lots of room for exercise.
SALUKI Generally healthy dog, a good family pet with no 'doggie' odour.	585–710 mm (23–28 in)	Lots	Smooth/ feathered	Regular	Good	Quite good	Retains its strong hunting instincts.
WHIPPET Shy and gentle. Easy to keep, hardy, and very loving to members of its own family.	470 mm (18½ in)	Lots	Short/fine	Little	Fair	Good	Retains its strong hunting instincts.

TERRIERS

Most of the terrier breeds originated in the British Isles, and their ancestors date back to the 15th century. In spite of their present diversity they all enjoy digging for vermin. The name Terrier is derived from terra, the Latin word for 'earth'. Because Terriers are in general small and compact, they have been readily accepted as house pets; most of the breeds get along well with children. The wiry coats of some terriers need special care, with regular stripping or trimming to keep them tidy. The typical terrier temperament, alert and quick, must be acceptable to you before you decide to take one of the group into your family circle.

Breed and character	Typical size of male	Amount of exercise	Coat type	Amount of grooming	Guarding potential	Temperament with children	Possible problems
AIREDALE TERRIER Called the King of the Terriers and once used as a war dog. Combines roles of pet and guard.	585–610 mm (23–24 in)	Lots	Hard/wiry	Regular	Excellent	Very good	Likes a scrap. Can be over-protective.
BORDER TERRIER Ideal working terrier and loving family pet. Good with other pets.	5·9–7 kg (13–15½ lb)	Lots	Harsh/dense	Little + occasional trim	Fair	Good	Needs surprising amount of space for its size.
BULL TERRIER Fearless, faithful, affectionate family dog: will protect the children with its life.	No limit	Lots	Flat/even	Little	Excellent	Very good	Very powerful for its size. Needs discipline when young.
CAIRN TERRIER Happy and friendly dog with boundless energy: a good companion.	6·4 kg (14 lb)	Lots	Hard/double	Regular + occasional trim	Fair	Good with own family	Very lively and needs lots of supervision.
FOX TERRIER, WIRE Faithful and intelligent. Very alert; not adverse to a scrap. Responds to careful training.	7·3–8·2 kg (16–18 lb)	Lots	Wiry	Regular + stripping	Quite good	Very good	Susceptible to eczema.
FOX TERRIER, SMOOTH Very smart and alert pet, and the perfect rat-catcher. Lively and intelligent.	7·3–8·2 kg (16–18 lb)	Lots	Hard/smooth	Regular	Quite good	Good with own family	Likes to scrap.
IRISH TERRIER Unusual bright coat. Alert and happy nature; devoted to its owner. Needs careful training.	460 mm (18 in)	Lots	Hard/wiry	Regular + stripping	Very good	Good	May be very disobedient off the lead. Likes a scrap.
JACK RUSSELL TERRIER Affectionate, sporty little dog not yet recognised as a breed by the Kennel Club. Economical to feed and needs little space.	No standard	Moderate	Variable	Regular	Fair	Quite good with own family	Excitable in the company of other dogs.
KERRY BLUE Very strong character. Ideal family dog if kept under control; can be fiercely protective.	460–485 mm (18–19 in)	Lots	Soft/profuse	Regular + trimming	Excellent	Very good	Likes a scrap. Needs firm handling when young.

The Airedale, known as 'King of the Terriers', is largest of his group.

Breed and character	Typical size of male	Amount of exercise	Coat type	Amount of grooming	Guarding potential	Temperament with children	Possible problems
NORFOLK AND NORWICH TERRIERS Very similar breeds: the Norfolk has dropped ears, the Norwich pricked ears. Good family pets, lovable, hardy, and fearless; adapt to any routine.	255 mm (10 in)	Moderate	Hard/wiry	Little	Good	Very good	Fearlessness may get them into trouble.
SCOTTISH TERRIER Loyal, honest, and reliable pet: home-loving and very protective. Ideal for retired people.	255–280 mm (10–11 in)	Moderate	Double	Regular + stripping	Very good	Fair	Dislikes most strangers. May be very sharp.
SEALYHAM TERRIER Needs careful early training. Becomes devoted to the family.	305 mm (12 in)	Lots	Long/wiry	Regular + stripping	Good	Good	Can be very obstinate. Likes a scrap.
WEST HIGHLAND WHITE TERRIER Happy, friendly family dog; loves other pets. Easy to train.	280 mm (11 in)	Moderate	Hard/wiry	Regular + stripping	Quite good	Very good	Can be obstinate.

TOYS

This group contains some of the most ancient breeds that were specially developed as companion and lap dogs. They were selected for diminutive size and unusual appearance rather than for their performance or skills. The members of this group may be divided into sub-groups related to the other main groups of dog breeds. Hounds, for example, are represented in miniature by the Italian Greyhound and the Spaniels by the Toy Spaniels and the Japanese Chin; terriers in the group are the Yorkshire Terrier and the English Toy Terrier. Some of the Toy breeds are hardy and strong despite their size, while others are fragile and easily damaged and are therefore unsuitable as family pets.

What they lack in size many of the Toys make up for in character and strength of personality, and they are ideal dogs as pets where space is at a premium. They are generally easy to train to toilet trays, and most of the breeds keep fit and healthy with a minimum of exercise.

Breed and character	Typical size of male	Amount of exercise	Coat type	Amount of grooming	Guarding potential	Temperament with children	Possible problems
BICHON FRISE Affectionate and happy pet, needing expert coat-care. Attractive and well-behaved.	Under 305 mm (1 in)	Moderate	Curly/ silky	Daily + trimming	Poor	Good	Expert care essential for keeping coat in condition.
CAVALIER KING CHARLES SPANIEL Gentle, very affectionate, and hardy. Likes other pets. A clean and attractive little dog.	5·5–8·2 kg (12–18 lb)	Moderate	Long/silky	Regular	Poor	Excellent	May need regular baths. Ears need special care.
CHIHUAHUA Intensely loyal and affectionate; intelligent. Is inclined to feel the cold.	0·9–2·7 kg (2–6 lb)	Little	Smooth — Long	Little — Regular	Poor, but barks fiercely	Fairly good	May snap if teased.
ITALIAN GREYHOUND Affectionate, obedient, and easy to train. Rarely moults; possesses no 'doggie' odour.	2·7–3·6 kg (6–8 lb)	Lots	Fine/ smooth	Little	Poor	Good	Very sensitive; feels the cold.
KING CHARLES SPANIEL More snub-nosed than Cavalier; hardy, healthy, and very affectionate. Likes other pets, and is easy to train.	3·6–6·4 kg (8–14 lb)	Moderate	Long/ straight	Daily	Poor	Very good	May need regular baths. Special attention to ears and eyes.
PEKINGESE Likes lots of fuss and petting. Aloof, but adores its own family.	Not exceeding 5 kg (11 lb)	Moderate	Long/ straight	Daily	Brave	Fair	Over-exertion causes breathing problems.
PUG Happy, intelligent, and loving pet; easy to manage. Tends to snore.	6·4–8·2 kg (14–18 lb)	Little	Short/fine	Little	Poor	Very good	Tends to overweight. Over-exertion causes breathing problems.
YORKSHIRE TERRIER Affectionate, quick to learn, and fearless. Ideal for apartment life.	Up to 3·2 kg (7 lb)	Little	Long/silky	Daily	Brave	Quite good	May need a weekly bath.

The perky Yorkshire Terrier, most popular small terrier breed in Britain.

WORKING DOGS

Although virtually all the breeds except the Toys were developed for some sort of work, most have been used for sporting pursuits. The Working group, however, includes all the non-sporting varieties. Dogs have been in the service of man for centuries as herders, fighting and war dogs, and for pack and haulage work. Today they are also trained for such refined duties as guiding the blind, protecting valuable property, and searching out drugs and explosives. Some of the working breeds have inbred temperaments that make them adaptable to life as family pets, but most still require a certain amount of work to do in order to prevent them from becoming bored. Most of the working breeds need lots of exercise and respond well to a high standard of obedience training.

Breed and character	Typical size of male	Amount of exercise	Coat type	Amount of grooming	Guarding potential	Temperament with children	Possible problems
BOXER Lively dog with a happy and exuberant nature; full of bounce and character. Needs correct training.	570–635 mm (22½–25 in)	Moderate	Short/close	Little	Very good	Very good	Boisterous. May enjoy a scrap.
COLLIE, BORDER. Intelligent and loyal: ideal choice for training to obedience level; very good general family dog.	535 mm (21 in)	Lots	Long/silky	Regular	Quite good	Good	Inclined to herd anything and everything.
COLLIE, ROUGH Very loyal and easy to train family dog.	560–610 mm (22–24 in)	Lots	Dense/straight	Lots	Quite good	Very good	May not like strangers.
DOBERMANN PINSCHER Fearless; needs careful and methodical training to counteract natural wilfulness.	685 mm (27 in)	Lots	Smooth/hard	Little	Excellent	Good with own family	May fight. Not keen on strangers.
GERMAN SHEPHERD DOG (ALSATIAN) Very good family dog when correctly raised: loyal, affectionate, and obedient.	610–660 mm (24–26 in)	Lots	Double	Regular	Excellent	Good with own family	Needs plenty to do and careful early training.
GREAT DANE Good-natured and very obedient when properly trained.	Min. 760 mm (30 in)	Little	Short/sleek	Little	Very good	Good with own family	Short-lived. Needs lots of space.
NORWEGIAN BUHUND Friendly and attractive little dog. A natural herder; loves to play with and protect children.	450 mm (17¾ in)	Lots	Close/harsh	Regular	Good	Excellent	Inclined to round-up other pets.
OLD ENGLISH SHEEPDOG Very intelligent; responds to training, and gets on well with other animals.	560 mm (22 in)	Lots	Shaggy/profuse	Lots + trimming	Very good	Excellent	Can be very boisterous; needs careful training.
ROTTWEILER Impressive and highly intelligent guard, and very reliable family dog; fearless.	635–685 mm (25–27 in)	Regular	Flat/coarse	Little	Excellent	Very good	Becomes very aggressive if kept chained.

The Samoyed, strong, hardy, and good natured, is typical of the larger Spitz breeds.

Breed and character	Typical size of male	Amount of exercise	Coat type	Amount of grooming	Guarding potential	Temperament with children	Possible problems
ST BERNARD Affectionate and very intelligent: easy to train.	Min. 695 mm (27½ in)	Regular	Dense/flat or short/ houndlike	Regular	Good	Very good with own family	Inclined to drool. Needs lots of space.
SAMOYED Beautiful-looking, loyal dog. Obedient and very intelligent, with an independent streak.	560 mm (22 in)	Lots	Thick/soft	Lots	Quite good	Fairly good	Sheds lots of white hair.
SHETLAND SHEEPDOG Intelligent and very faithful pet: trains well up to obedience standard. A neat, quiet housedog.	370 mm (14½ in)	Moderate	Double	Lots	Fairly good	Fairly good	Dislikes strangers.
WELSH CORGI Hardy and tireless pet, very loyal to own family but with little time for strangers.	255–305 mm (10–12 in)	Moderate	Short/ hard	Little	Good	Quite good	May be hostile to strangers. Needs careful training – is inclined to nip.

UTILITY DOGS

Breed and character	Typical size of male	Amount of exercise	Coat type	Amount of grooming	Guarding potential	Temperament with children	Possible problems
BOSTON TERRIER Neat and very attractive dog with a very strong character. Rarely sheds coat; free from 'doggie' odour.	Up to 11·3 kg (25 lb)	Little	Smooth/ fine	Little	Good	Excellent	Prone to eye problems.
BULLDOG Lovable and very courageous. Intelligent, and easy to train. An enthusiast's breed.	25 kg (55 lb)	Little	Fine/short	Little	Good	Very good	Snores. Rather short-lived.
DALMATIAN Long-lived and lively. Responds to careful discipline when young. Good-natured and intelligent.	610 mm (24 in)	Lots	Hard/ dense	Moderate	Quite good	Very good	Sheds coat. May be deaf. Needs careful training.

The Bulldog, despite its fierce appearance, makes an affectionate family pet.

This very diverse group seems to contain dogs of all shapes and sizes which do not fit readily into any other group. Most of the breeds can be classed as Companion Dogs. Some were first bred for working purposes; the Poodle, for example, is descended from the Old Water Dog, a fine sporting breed. Whatever your preference in size, shape, general appeal, coat texture, or character, there must surely be a dog to suit your needs as a family pet among those listed as Utility.

Breed and character	Typical size of male	Amount of exercise	Coat type	Amount of grooming	Guarding potential	Temperament with children	Possible problems
LHASA APSO Attractive and amusing little dog with lots of character. Very active, responsive to training. Confident and engaging.	255 mm (10 in)	Moderate	Long/ straight	Lots	Fairly good	Excellent	Suspicious of strangers.
POODLE, STANDARD Intelligent, affectionate, and very responsive to training. Best with older children.	over 380 mm (15 in)	Lots	Curly/ profuse	Trimming + expert grooming	Quite good	Good	Must be taken seriously: it resents teasing.
POODLE, MINIATURE Intelligent, affectionate, and very responsive to training. Best with older children.	Not under 280 mm (11 in) Not over 380 mm (15 in)	Moderate	Curly/ profuse	Trimming + expert grooming	Quite good	Quite good	Sensitive. Noisy unless checked.
SCHIPPERKE Hardy dog of handy size. Affectionate and very loyal.	5·5–7·3 kg (12–16 lb)	Little	Dense/ harsh	Little	Very good	Very good	Needs a lot of individual attention.
SCHNAUZER, STANDARD Good-natured, lively and very playful pet; terrier-like in behaviour. Very alert and protective.	485 mm (19 in)	Lots	Hard/wiry	Regular + trimming	Excellent	Very good	Notoriously distrustful of strangers.
SCHNAUZER, MINIATURE Very quick to learn and easily trained. A long-lived pet.	355 mm (14 in)	Moderate	Hard/wiry	Regular + trimming	Very good	Good	Shares its larger relative's dislike of strangers.
SHIH-TZU Delightful pet that adores its family. Has a very arrogant manner. Highly intelligent.	Up to 265 mm (10½ in)	Little	Long/ dense	Lots	Poor	Very good	Prone to eye troubles. You can mitigate these to some extent by tying back its topknot.
TIBETAN SPANIEL Perfect family pet, happy, intelligent, and with an independent streak which gives it great character.	255 mm (10 in)	Moderate	Double	Regular	Poor	Very good	Coat may need extra care, and in any case must be brushed at least once a day.
TIBETAN TERRIER Delightful character and happy disposition. Easy to train.	355–405 mm (14–16 in)	Moderate	Double	Lots	Good	Very good	Shaggy coat needs extra care.

Index

Page numbers in *italics* refer to captions

ACKNOWLEDGEMENTS
The publishers wish to thank the following for their kind permission to reproduce the photographs in this book:
Animal Graphics/Solitaire 10–11, 16, 18, 22, 28–9, 30–1, 44–53; Animal Photography/Sally Anne Thompson 54, 69, 70, 73, 78; Bruce Coleman Ltd (John Markham) 75, (Reinhard 66–7, 77; Ian McLean 2–3, 20–1, 38, 63; John Moss 14–15, 27, 32–3; Spectrum Colour Library 23, 35; Dr Michael Woodhouse 42–3; Zefa Picture Library (Reinhard/Tierfoto) 40, (Revers-Widaner) 55
Special Photography John Moss 1, 4–5, 6–7, 8–9, 13, 36–7, 39, 41, 56–7, 59, 60–1, 62, 64–5.
Illustrators Russell Barnet 49, 53, 58, 60, 63; Hayward and Martin 12, 17; David Nockels, The Garden Studio 24, 25, 68, 71, 72–3, 74, 76–7, 78–9; Stan North 18, 19, 26

The author thanks Peter Dollemore of East Grinstead for his training advice, and Sally Zing for demonstrating training methods with Norwulf Yankee Gal.